"Ever' Texan oughta r
 – Glenn Dromgoole, *Abile*

STORIES FROM TEXAS

Some of Them Are True

By W. F. Strong

BERKELEY PLACE BOOKS

This book is dedicated to my precocious 3-year-old daughter, Scarlett Paloma-Maria Strong, who has taught me that stories are best told on tippy-toes, with hands stretched high and a mouth full of chocolate.

Stories From Texas: Some of Them Are True
By W.F. Strong
Cover photo: Wyman Meinzer
Editor: Amy Culbertson
Book designer: Tom Johanningmeier
Cover designer: Jared Stone

1st edition
10 9 8 7 6 5 4 3 2

Bulk sales of books from Berkeley Place Books are available at special discounts for fundraising, promotions and premiums.

Berkeley Place Books
An imprint of Great Texas Line Press
Post Office Box 11105
Fort Worth, Texas 76110
817-922-8929 / FAX 817-926-0420

Printed in USA by Versa Press, East Peoria, Ill.

Library of Congress Cataloging-in-Publication Data
Strong, W.F., 1952
Stories From Texas: Some of Them Are True / by W.F. Strong
144 p. cm.

ISBN 978-1-892588-661 (original paperback)
1. Texas 2. Texana 3. Texas folklore 4. Texas culture 5. Texas history 6. Texas humor 7. Texas speech 8. Texas writers 9. Judge Roy Bean 10. Blue Bell Ice Cream 11. Van Cliburn 12. Robert Duvall 13. Charles Goodnight 14. Elmer Kelton 15. King Ranch 16. Tom Landry 17. "Lonesome Dove" 18. Larry McMurtry 19. Quanah Parker 20. "The Texas Chainsaw Massacre" 21. Mark Twain 22. Whataburger

CONTENTS

INTRODUCTION

WELCOME TO TEXAS AND MY STORIES

Many books are unintentional: We don't start out to write a book; the book simply evolves of its own will. That is how this one came about.

In the beginning, I just wanted to share moving passages from books I had read about Texas. I wanted fellow Texans, and admirers of Texas, to experience the beauty and sublimity of Texas writers like McMurtry, McCarthy and Meyer; Dobie and Haley; Kelton and Bedichek; Ivins and Hale. I wanted them to know our literature and our folklore and to appreciate the lesser-known stories of our history.

So I persuaded a local NPR station to let me "tell some stories" about Texas in four minutes or less. Chris Maley and Mario Munoz of Rio Grande Valley Public Radio agreed to let me try, and *Stories From Texas* was born. Seven years later, here I am, publishing a collection of 75 of these radio stories, adapted, edited and in some cases expanded for print.

This wouldn't have happened if other stations hadn't also picked up *Stories From Texas*. In 2012, Matt Meinke of KETR in Commerce started airing them. The next year, David Woo of KTEP in El Paso started playing them. Then, in 2014, I got a call from Emily Donahue, who was managing editor at the *Texas Standard* in Austin. She asked if I would be willing to do some commentaries for their award-winning network of some 30 NPR stations. I said I would be most honored to come on board.

Naturally, that kind of exposure led to letters and suggestions from all over Texas about new stories I might tell. The one thing I have learned in all this is that Texans deeply love Texas. It's not that I didn't know that before, but I don't think I realized how deep that affection lies or how common it is among the vast majority of Texans, regardless of ethnicity. In fact, I think Texans are a distinct ethnicity, the way the Basque of northern Spain are a distinct culture within Spain, the way the Bavarians are Bavarians first and Germans second. You don't have to share genetics to be a Texan, you just have to share a cultural view. As Steinbeck said, "Texas is a state of mind . . . it is a mystique, closely approximating a religion."

So in this collection of stories I have attempted to cover the rich cultural heritage of Texas in categories that focus on a variety of things: the Texas dialect and its unique nature; larger-than-life Texans like Charles Goodnight and Tom Landry; Texas writers and writings about Texas; iconic Texas brands, from Whataburger to Blue Bell. I've included some classic modern folklore one could share over drinks at happy hour, as well as some personal memories.

If all goes as planned, you should find plenty of laughter here and maybe even a tear or two, and you might learn something you hadn't known about this fascinating and various state. You'll also find a little melancholic longing for a Texas that once was but can never be again. But time moves on, and there are great years yet to be lived by new generations who have inherited a powerful cultural DNA from their ancestors. They will work their own magic within their own times.

— *W.F. Strong*

DEFINING A TEXAN

Not long ago, I met an old rodeo cowboy in the Live Oak County town of George West. We were discussing how you know if someone's a real Texan.

He said, "Well, I think all you gotta do is ask a few questions."

Intrigued, I asked, "Like what kind of questions?"

"Well," he said, "like this:"

You ever seen the big Texas sun rise up over the oil derricks of the Gulf, and turn 'em to gold, and found that beautiful?

You ever laid back on Emory Peak, under the starry skies of Big Bend, and reached up and touched God's first day's work?

You ever driven the country roads just to see the wildflowers celebrating spring, or floated down the Guadalupe with a cold beer on hot summer's day?

Ever eaten three-alarm chili in Terlingua …

… tamped down with pan de campo?

Ever eat a Dilley watermelon, or Poteet strawberries, or Hill Country or Parker County peaches so good they made you cry?

You got Blue Bell in your freezer right now?

Is Southwest, to you, the National Airline of Texas?

Do you feel a gnawing sadness when you leave the state and a reborn joy when you make it back?

Ever had beef enchiladas on the River Walk …

… chicken-fried steak with cream gravy in Abilene …

… or a Shiner Bock in Shiner?

You ever see Staubach or Aikman bring the 'Boys back from the dead?

Ever see Earl Campbell run like a blustery wind in the Astrodome, or Nolan Ryan pitch a heart-stoppin' no-hitter?

Do you know that Houston is the "world's doctor"?

Are you equally comfortable with 'hola' and 'howdy'?

Do you like jalapeños on your Whataburger? For breakfast?

Does Austin seems normal to you?

Ever seen Willie play live in Luckenbach?

Do you love the smell of orange blossoms on the March wind, or purple sage after a thunderstorm?

Is Lonesome Dove *the best miniseries there ever was?*

Is your favorite president Sam Houston?

Did you ever sit in reverent silence at the Alamo in gratitude for the gift they gave?

You ever drive through the gritty haze of a West Texas sandstorm, spurred on by ZZ Top?

Do you love a second helping of Frito Pie under Friday night lights?

Do you cheer the bronc rider and the running back with equal fervor?

Ever ridden your horse through the Dairy Queen drive-through?

Ever go to spring break at South Padre and woke up face-down in beer-soaked sand, or partied in a border town till you couldn't find the bridge?

You have a Lone Star flag flying in your yard?

Is HEB your pantry?

Do you see yourself as a Texan first and just incidentally American?

Did you smile when you learned that the Texas Capitol was taller than the one in Washington?

You think mesquite smoke makes everything taste better?

When America the Beautiful *plays, do you think about Texas?*

"If you can say 'yes' to most all these things," the cowboy said, "then you have the right, the honor, to proudly call yourself a Texan."

I think the ol' boy had a point.

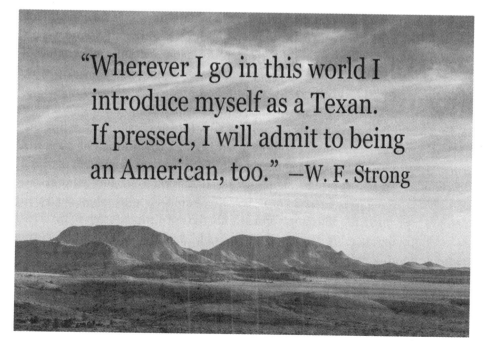

"Wherever I go in this world I introduce myself as a Texan. If pressed, I will admit to being an American, too." —W. F. Strong

Photo by Jeff Lynch

MY 10 FAVORITE QUOTES ABOUT TEXAS

In no particular order:

1. Davy Crockett: *"You may all go to hell, and I will go to Texas."*
Crockett said this angrily after losing his Tennessee bid for the U.S. Congress. (I think he really said, "Y'all can go to hell," but grammatical purity likely corrupted the original transcription.)

2. Mary Lasswell: *"I am forced to conclude that God made Texas on his day off, for pure entertainment, just to prove that all that diversity could be crammed into one section of earth by a really top hand."*
Author Mary Lasswell grew up in Brownsville and wrote a number of popular novels and other works, including the book *I'll Take Texas.*

3. John Gunther: *"If a man's from Texas, he'll tell you. If not, why embarrass him by asking?"*
Many people think Gunther was a big gruff Texas oilman. He wasn't. He was a famous journalist whose "Inside" series — including *Inside U.S.A.,* the source of this quote — was hugely popular in the '30s and '40s.

4. Wallace O. Chariton: *"In the covered-wagon days, if a baby was born in Texarkana while the family was crossing into the Lone Star State, by the time they reached El Paso, the baby would be in the third grade."*
Texana writer Chariton came up with this colorful reference to the size of Texas. Please don't do the math on this and write to tell me that at 10 miles a day this trip would only take three months. There is nothing to be gained from viewing Texas hyperbole through a lens of realism.

5. Conrad Hilton: *"There's a vastness here, and I believe that the people who are born here breathe that vastness into their soul. They dream big dreams and think big thoughts, because there is nothing to hem them in."*
Hilton launched his empire in Texas with his very first hotel in Cisco in 1919, going on to open Hiltons in Dallas, Abilene, Waco and El Paso before expanding beyond the state.

6. Larry McMurtry: *"What my whole body of work says . . . is that Texans spent so long getting past the frontier experience because that experience is so overwhelmingly powerful. Imagine yourself as a small hopeful* *immigrant family, alone on the Staked Plains, with the Comanche and the Kiowa still on the loose. The power of such experience will not sift out of the descendants of that venturer in one generation and produce Middletown. Elements of that primal venturing will surely inform several generations."*

McMurtry wrote this in an essay on Texas cities for *Texas Monthly* several years ago. In more accessible language, he also famously said: "Only a rank degenerate would drive 1500 miles across Texas without eating a chicken-fried steak."

7. **James Michener:** *"What you Northerners never appreciate . . . is that Texas is so big that you can live your life within its limits and never give a damn about what anyone in Boston or San Francisco thinks . . . A writer can build a perfectly satisfactory reputation in Texas and he doesn't give a damn about what critics in Kalamazoo think. His universe is big enough to gratify any ambition. Same with businessmen. Same with newspapers. Same with everything."*

This is from Michener's 1985 blockbuster *Texas*.

8. **George W. Bush, reflecting poignantly on his years in West Texas:** *"Those were comfortable, carefree years. The word I'd use now is idyllic. On Friday nights, we cheered on the Bulldogs of Midland High. On Sunday mornings, we went to church. Nobody locked their doors. Years later, when I would speak about the American Dream, it was Midland I had in mind."*

9. **John Steinbeck:** *"I have said that Texas is a state of mind, but I think it is more than that. It is a mystique closely approximating a religion. And this is true to the extent that people either passionately love Texas or passionately hate it and, as in other religions, few people dare to inspect it for fear of losing their bearings in mystery or paradox. But I think there will be little quarrel with my feeling that Texas is one thing. For all its enormous range of space, climate, and physical appearance, and for all the internal squabbles, contentions, and strivings, Texas has a tight cohesiveness perhaps stronger than any other section of America. Rich, poor, Panhandle, Gulf, city, country, Texas is the obsession, the proper study and the passionate possession of all Texans."*

This is perhaps my favorite Texas quote of all. It is from Steinbeck's memoir *Travels With Charley: In Search of America*.

10. **And we must hear from Molly Ivins, too:** *"I think provincialism is an endemic characteristic with mankind. I think everyone everywhere is provincial. But it is particularly striking with Texans, and we tend to be very Tex-centric."*

THE TEXAS DIALECT AND TEX-CENTRIC TENDENCIES

TALKIN' TEXAN:
THE TELLTALE TEXAS DIPHTHONG

A nice lady wrote to me not long ago and said that she was happy to have a son with a good solid, two-syllable Texas name. "His name is Ben," she wrote.

I loved that. We do that, don't we? Well, many of us do, anyway. There are 30 million Texans, so there are many dialects out there. But in the traditional or classic Texas dialect, we tend to convert one-syllable words to two-syllable words. Ben becomes "Bey-uhn." Jet becomes "Jay-ut." Mess is "May-us." This is what I call the Texas Diphthong.

And, believe it or not, some of us are so talented we can create a triphthong out of a one-syllable word. We can squeeze three into one. Ham becomes "Ha-uh-um." This talent has been particularly mastered by televangelists who really like to elongate those vowels with words like 'hell,' which becomes "hay-uhl-ah." Sounds more frightening that way. When they say it like that it doesn't differ from the hail that falls from the sky — so I'm not sure whether they are talking about fire or ice.

And that is something typical of us Texans. We make no distinction between some sounds that people up north make a big distinction between. We make no distinction between the pen that we write with and the flag pin we wear on our suits. Up north they say "Bic pen" with a short e and "flag pin" with a short i. We say the Bic-type pen and the flag-type pin the same way, with a short i. Perfect rhyme. Up North they say "beer" and "bear" differently. Some Texans make no distinction between the bear they run from and the beverage they drink to celebrate getting away.

I got many of these examples from my friend Dr. Lars Hinrichs, who is a professor of linguistics at Austin's University of Texas — a word doctor. For years he has been studying Texas English, and he tells me that in the I-35 corridor we are seeing a leveling of the accent. This means that the mingling of all the newcomers' accents with ours is causing phonetic hybrids to emerge. So the classic Texas dialect, in the corridor, is not quite as strong as it was 20 years ago. It is evolving. Compared to the corridor, though, East Texas and West Texas are leveling at a glacial pace Also, y'all will be happy to know that "y'all," according to Dr. Hinrichs, is not receding. It is perhaps proliferating because it is so grammatically efficient. All y'all newcomers are pickin' it up. Some linguists say that even Californians and the New Yorkers have started to use it.

Hollywood has had its struggles with the Texas accent, often hiring dialogue coaches for authenticity. When Michael Caine came to Texas to film *Secondhand Lions*, he was having trouble mastering the Texas accent. His dialogue coach, he said, taught him that Texans let their words lean up against each other. Caine said he realized that British English is clipped, crisp and precise, while Texas English is relaxed: Each word leans into the next one and just keeps things goin' along smoothly. He learned to spread out his vowels and let his consonants lean up against each other. That's it. That's the secret. I won't say he mastered it, but I will say *Secondhand Lions* was a fine Texas film.

So the Texas accent is in no danger of dyin' out. But I do think we should make an effort to keep it from becoming endangered. Wouldn't want to have to start a Foundation for the Endangered Texas Accent. FETA. So we can prevent that by all y'all makin' sure you use "y'all" a dozen times a day and always be fixin' to do somethin'. Get relaxed with your language. Let your words lean up against each other. And make sure you use your Texas Diphthong every chance you "gee-ut."

TALKIN' TEXAN: LETTERS WE DON'T NEED

In the classic Texas English dialect, there are a good number of letters you don't need. You can get rid of 'em. That's a case in point right there: You can dispense with the "th" in "them": *Get rid of 'em.* There's a wonderful hybrid word built around " 'em," and it is "Momnem," short, of course, for "Momma and them": *We're goin' for supper over at Momnem's house.*

If I were teaching a non-native Texan to speak in the classic Texas dialect, this is what I'd say:

First, eliminate all the "g"s on the "-ing" endings. If you're wantin' to get to talkin' like a classic Texan, eliminatin' your "g"s is a good start.

You also want to dispense with the "a" on "appreciate." Just say, "Preciate it": *Preciate all you've done for us, partner. Preciate your droppin' by for a visit.* You can drop out the "A" in "American," too. Just say "Merican." Similarly, you can toss out the "e" in "especially": *I bought this specially for you. I'm not specially hungry right now. Couldn't be true, specially considering I wudn't even there.*

Next you can confidently ditch the "e" on "enough": *'Nuff said.*

To sound like a classic Texan, you will want to take the final "w" off of "window" and "pillow." Then switch out that "o" for an "a." Say "winda" and "pilla": *Can you hand me the pilla that's over by the winda?*

Now ditch the "d" on "iced tea." Even when it is written, in many restaurants, the "d" is nowhere to found. So we just say "ice tea," and some Texans squeeze the words together to make it one: "icetea." Rhymes with "feisty" that way. (Although many Texans dispense with the "ice" altogether and just ask for "tea," because tea is assumed to be iced by default; hot tea is not an imaginable option.)

You can generally dispense with the "a" in "about": *How 'bout we go see a movie? How 'bout them Cowboys?* We have said "How 'bout them Cowboys!" so long we have forgotten that it's grammatically wrong. It should be "How about those Cowboys," of course, but that is just nerd grammar: So right it's wrong.

Another serious grammatical sin, in some people's eyes, is "ain't," originally the contraction of "am not" that has come to be used for "are not," "is not" and sometimes "has not" or "have not" as well. This one comes down to us from Cockney slang in early 19th-century England, which is why it came to be considered uneducated slang. But "ain't" is used often between the most educated of Texans as a bond of friendship: *You ain't seen nothin' yet, buddy.* I'm reminded of the great baseball player and sports broadcaster Dizzy Dean, who pitched for the Houston Buffaloes in the Texas League before making the majors. Taken to task for using "ain't" in his broadcasts, he famously noted that there were a lot of people "ain't usin' ain't ain't eatin."

TEXAS CONTRACTIONS

Anytime I hear someone say something like this: "Y'all 'bout fixin' to head out?" I think it's highly likely that they are from Texas. You have *"y'all"* and *"fixin' to"* in the same sentence.

We do love our contractions, which, if you don't recall from your halcyon days of grammar school, are words squeezed together to make one shorter word, with apostrophes standing in for what's missing. And "y'all," of course, is our most famous contraction — it's heard throughout the South, but we Texans are particularly fond of it — probably owing to its extreme usefulness, since proper English inexplicably does not offer us a distinction between the second person singular and the second person plural, both being "you."

But we have even extended its usefulness by placing "all" in front of it to form "all y'all." It is well known that "y'all" describes two or more and that "all y'all" could mean five or 500. "Y'all" might refer to your immediate family, say — whoever lives in your house — and "all y'all" to one's extended family, grandparents, aunts, cousins and the like. Or "y'all" could be the group you came to the party with, while "all y'all" might be used to address everybody at the party. We even use "y'all" possessively, as in "y'all's." I heard this sentence at a barbecue not long ago: "Y'all need to move all y'all's trucks so Carlos can leave."

Now that y'all have heard this, I know y'all are gonna start wanting to practice your possessives, but try to wait till the lesson is finished. I'll let you go in two minutes.

The king of contractions, I believe, is "y'all'd've." It has three apostrophes in it. Three! You have to admire the muscular nature of that contraction: Y'all'd've. *You all would have.* And here's how you use it: "Y'all'd've loved it if y'all'd've come." Now just stand back and take in the magnificence of that sentence. Twelve words reduced to 6! That, ladies and gentlemen, is the very soul of linguistic efficiency.

Less spectacular cousins of "y'all'd've" are "she'd've" and "he'd've": *I figure she'd've married him if he wudn't such a ne'er-do-well.* Or, for a more modern take: *He'd've already lost 20 pounds if he'd've stuck with that low-carb diet.*

Texans — older ones, especially, can also use an interesting contraction for something that is owned by at least two people: *"Whose dog is this?" "Oh, that Yorkie is our'n."* "Our'n" may or may not be a contraction of "our own"; it goes all the way back to Middle English and no doubt got to Texas via Appalachia, where, along with "his'n," her'n" and "your'n," it has been a bit slower to die out than it has here. The expression is a bit archaic — on its last legs, so to speak — but can still be heard in Texas if you listen carefully.

That's our linguistics lesson for today. Y'all'd've liked it a lot more if y'all'd've been listening instead of repeating everything for your immediate amusement, but that's okay. As long as all y'all had a good time.

MISPRONUNCIATING IN TEXAS

I've been keeping a list of the most commonly mispronounced words in Texas. Well, they aren't absolutely unique to Texas; many are Southernisms, but they are certainly common in Texas. And this is not to say that *all* Texans mispronounce *all* these words, or to say that their mispronunciation is exclusively Texan, but it is to say that some of us Texans mispronounce all of them and most of us mispronounce some of them.

In no particular order, here we go:

- "BRAY-mer," for the cattle breed brought to Texas from India in the mid-1800s: *I'd be careful around that big Braymer bull if I was you.* The correct name of the breed is, of course, Brahman, pronounced "BRAH-muhn," but somewhere along the way in Texas the "n" was dropped, an "r" added and that first "a" lengthened.

- "Waterburger." It is, of course, pronounced "WHAT-a-burger," but many of us prefer "Waterburger": *Can I get two Waterburgers with cheese, and could you Watersize the fries?*

- "Bob wire" or "bob war." It is actually "barbed wire," but many of us, especially those of us having intimate acquaintance with it on a daily basis, say "bob wire."

- Closely aligned with this is "chesterdrawers," for "chest of drawers." I was about 18 before I knew the true spelling of these two phrases. Before that I just thought Bob made wire and Chester made drawers.

- Then there's "probably": We like to ditch at least one "b" and say "prob-ly." But some of us get rid of both "b"s and just say "prawly." *You goin' to the dance tonight? I reckon' so, prawly.*

- Many in the older generations say "warsh" instead of "wash." *George Warshington. Warshington, D.C.* They warsh the clothes and the dishes, too.

- "Libery" instead of "library" is quite common. Reminds me of the hoary old story of the Texan who went up there to Harvard and stopped a Harvard man on the campus and asked, "Can you tell me where the libery's at?" Came the reply: "Here at Harvard, we say 'library,' not 'libery,' and we do not end our sentences in prepositions." So the Texan says, "Excuse me. Can you tell me where the library's at, jackass?"

- "Dreckly" for "directly": *I'll do it dreckly.* Contrary to what you might think, "dreckly"/"directly" does not mean immediately, but rather, "As soon as I get around to it."

- "Purty" is commonly used for "pretty," even used oxymoronically, as in "She's purty ugly." *Sorry to tell you, but that old truck of yours is lookin' purty ugly.*

- "Purt'-near" for "pretty near": *I reckon I'll be purt'-near finished with that fence by suppertime tomorrow.*

- Some of us, including President George W. Bush, say "nucular" instead of nuclear. *Can't let them Russkies get more nucular arms than we got.*

- Texans say "dudn't and wudn't" for "doesn't" and "wasn't": *He dudn't need to worry about not invitin' me 'cuz I wudn't gonna go in the first place!*

- "Thang" for "thing" is another one, and "everything" is "ever-thang." *Hand me that thang over there.*

- "Calvary" for "cavalry." When people need help they send for the cavalry, not the Calvary. Calvary is the name of the hill where Jesus was crucified.

- "Kindly" for "kind of" (or for "kinda"): *He looked kindly peaked.* ("Peak-ed," by the way, is pronounced "PEEK-id," in much the same way that "naked" is often pronounced "NECK-id," and it means ill or gaunt.

• "SaLmon." The "l" in salmon is properly silent. So don't ask for smoked saLmon. However, if you order in Spanish, or Italian, you can use the "l" and all is well.

• We may add an "h" at the end of "height," making it "heighth": *What's his heighth, about 6-2?* This may come from trying to be consistent with "width" and "breadth." Or maybe not, since we sometimes do the same thing with "sheath cake" for the popular one-layer chocolate dessert called Texas sheet cake.

• When we are not adding "h"s, we take some away. Many Texans lose the "H" on Houston and just say "YOU-ston": *Goin' down to Youston this weekend.*

• You might hear a woman say, "My husband takes me for granite." We do have a lot of granite in Texas. The Capitol is made of granite, quarried from Granite Mountain near Marble Falls. But the expression is "taken for granted," not "taken for granite," which might be worse.

• "Tia-juana." *Went down to Tia-juana for my niece's wedding. Came back with the Tia-juana two-step.* It's actually just Tijuana: No extra "a." When you say "Tia-juana" you are saying "Aunt Juana." Of course, Texans have been mangling Spanish words for centuries, so this is only one example of many.

That's my latest list of mispronunciations, but don't think I'm being unduly pedantic. As soon as I'm off the radio I'm likely to slip back into some of these comfortable long vowels and lazy consonants myself.

THE NATIONAL VERB OF TEXAS

"Fixin' to" is the national verb of Texas. Certainly you find it in use in other states, but it is particularly pervasive in Texas. For many of us, it is the default verb for anything to do with the near future. And most of us replace that final "o" with an "a": "Fixin' ta." As my mom would say, "I'm fixin' ta vacuum in there, so y'all don't get too comfortable."

"Fixin to" is about three things:

• Intentionality: something we intend to do, which is why so little gets done in many homes. We are always fixin' to and not actually fixin'. Congress sometimes has the same problem: Always fixin' to fix something but not fixin' it.

• Contemplation: *Hold your horses, Martha, I'm fixin' to decide.*

• Forewarning: *I'm fixin' to get mad here in a minute.*

If you told me I couldn't use "fixin' to," like many Texans I would be grammatically paralyzed for a while. I have no backup at this position. I have no other verb sitting on the on the bench ready to go in. Oh, I could send in "preparing to," or "getting ready to," but neither of those is as good a grammatical scrambler as "fixin' to" is. Fixin' to has it all: It can run, pass, stall for time and run out the clock.

For instance, I asked my brother Redneck Dave if he had fixed the mower I dropped at his house last week. He said:

"I was fixin' to fix it this mornin', but I decided to fix breakfast first 'cuz I saw all these fixin's I knew would make a fine omelet, so right now I'm fixin' to eat, but when I finish, I'm fixin' to look for my tools. If I can find 'em, I'll get started on fixin' your mower."

You have to stand in awe of that sentence for its sheer dexterity and work avoidance.

Obviously, the word "fix" has utility beyond "fixin' to." Let's break it down by tense:

Past tense: "I done fixed it," which is rare because mostly we're merely planning to fix things.

Conditional tense: "I might coulda fixed it if he hadn't tried to fix it first, but now it's fixed for good."

Future: "Soon as I finish this beer, I'm fixin' to think of a way to fix that for you."

And then there is this beautiful mash-up of present and future that doesn't have a name, really. It is a pure Southern hybrid: "I'm fixin' to fix it."

And now I'm fixin' ta wrap up this commentary by leaving you with the best bit of folk wisdom ever uttered about the word "fix." "If it ain't broke, don't fix it."

MIGHT OUGHTA TALK ABOUT TEXAS GRAMMAR

In Texas we are mighty big on the word "mighty." "Mighty" is used as a ubiquitous adjective: *Mighty pretty, mighty ugly, mighty expensive,* etc.

The word "might" is popular, too. It is used in place of maybe. Instead of saying, "Maybe I can help you Sunday," we say, "I might could help you on Sunday." "Might" works with verbs to give us an impressive menu of options for conditional expressions like *might could, might better, might oughta, might've used to,* and even the steroidal conditional tense: *might woulda had oughta.*

Taken out of context, these phrases can sound odd and even wrong, but when heard in conversation, they come to life and seem, well, mighty normal to many of us. I want to point out that Texas is a diverse state of varied dialects, so I will not claim that all of these conjugations are common. Some are and some aren't. Some I heard as a young man in south and west Texas but hear only rarely now, if ever.

Many Texans would never use this kind of folksy grammar, but there are many who prefer its unadorned utility. And there are many who would never talk this way at work but slip into these comfortable rhythms when they get home. Some of us are bi-dialectal.

• Let's begin with "might could." It is often used to answer a question:

"Would you go with me to the movies Friday night?" "Might could."

"You figure you can fix the starter on my truck?" "Might could."

• "Might would better," which in my younger days I heard used among oilfield men, has a good deal of appeal. It is most often used as a command. You occasionally hear it in Western movies:

"Sheriff, you might would better think long and hard 'fore you pick up that gun."

Or you can use it as a self-directed, thinking-out-loud, suggestion:

"Well, I might would better get on to bed. Long day tomorrow."

"Might would better" is also a future-tense conditional verb, referring to something that might be done differently in the near future:

"On second thought, I think they might would better drive on down here Friday night."

"Tell you what, she might would better just divorce that man."

• "Might oughta" is often used in the sense of shaking one's head over poor choices:

"She might oughta thought about those bills before she quit a job without havin' another."

"He might oughta known not to tease a rattlesnake, especially with a short stick."

• For an uncertain memory, we have "might have used to."

"I might have used to stay there when I was in Dallas, but I can't say for certain. "

"I think I might have used to know how many feet was in a mile, but now that you ask, I can't recall."

• And here's the mighty king of the conditional tense: "might woulda had oughta." Linguists call this modal stacking, like verbal Legos — just keep piling on verbs to see how high you can stack them. "Might woulda had oughta" is way outside the bounds of standard English.

When my wife, an English prof and proud member of the Grammar Police, hears such verbal anarchy, she wants to call in the swat team. But I find "might woulda had oughta" admirably creative. It's like watching LeBron James fly to the basket and do a midair spin to reverse dunk between two defenders. Magic.

In redneck culture, this is comfort grammar:

"They might woulda had oughta sold that house about ten years ago before

it fell apart on 'em."

"They might woulda had oughta listened to me when I told 'em not to buy a used pickup that was owned by a teenager."

• The famous Southern linguist Jeff Foxworthy has pointed out how useful "used to could" is in Southern speech. Like when people ask, "Do you dance?" and some respond: "Used to could."

"Used to could" is often used in modal stacking. "Might have" often precedes it:

"You know how to program the TV remote?" "Might have used to could, but not anymore."

See? Saves you from unwanted work. Here's another instructive example:

"Can you tune up my '98 GMC Z-71?" "Well, I might have used to could, but I'm mighty doubtful about it now."

MEASURING LIKE A TEXAN: YONDER AND SMIDGEN

There are two types of measurement systems in the world: metric and imperial. Metric is used by all but three countries (although some remnants of the latter linger in the UK). The remaining three officially use the imperial system, also known as British Imperial, employing inches, feet, miles; pints, quarts and gallons; and ounces and pounds as units.

These three backwater countries are Liberia, Myanmar and the United States of America. In Texas, we often use an even more informal Southern System for distance and weight, one that I like to call "Yonder and Smidgen." Yonder is for distance, smidgen for weight or amount.

I have found there are two kinds of people in Texas: those who say "yonder," and those over yonder, who don't.

"Yonder" is highly diverse in its meanings. It can be used for nearby: *"Put this down yonder at the other end of the table."*

It can be in or out, or even over.

For down the hall: *"I'm goin' in yonder to the TV room."*

For in the yard: *"Could you go out yonder and get the paper?"*

Or for across town: *"Gotta drive over yonder to H.E.B."*

Or it can be used for great distances, such as: *"Can't believe they drove all the way out yonder to Arizona just for a birthday party."*

Just change the preposition and you have adjusted for distance — down yonder, in yonder, out yonder, over yonder, way out yonder. And let's not forget the wild blue yonder and the ultimate "up yonder," where we all want to be when the roll is called.

I guess the greatest distance Texans regularly cope with is Texas herself.

So when yonder won't do, we have this: "The sun did rise and the sun did set and I ain't out of Texas yet."

Another informal distance you hear often in Texas is "damnear":

"The way he swung that axe he damnear took my head off."

"If you wanna buy beer, you're gonna have to drive damnear to Dallas, or damnear into next week."

I had a great-uncle long ago who used to measure distance in beer. *"It's about a two-beer drive."* I'm not endorsing, just reporting.

And for very short distances we have "If it had been a snake it would've bit you."

Then for density we have "Couldn't throw a rock without hittin' …": *"You can't throw a rock in Austin without hittin' a lawyer."*

Or for small and cramped we have, "That room was so small you couldn't swing a cat in there." Why you would want to swing a cat I have never figured out. I doubt cats favor the custom either.

For amounts we have a smidgen. It is mostly used in cooking: *"Just put a smidgen more of garlic in there and the beans will be perfect."*

For larger amounts, bucketful: *"How many nails you need?"* "Bring a bucketful." Or: *"He ain't worth a bucketful of warm spit."*

Wish we could discuss oilfield measurements, but things would get indelicate quickly.

Well, I wanted to talk about measurements of time, too. But I don't have time for time. I've got to drive over yonder to the bank faster than small-town gossip to make a deposit before they close. Gotta go so fast I'll likely catch up with yesterday. Adios.

DEMONYMS OF TEXAS

For a month before writing this I was deep into demonymology. Sounds ominous, but it is not the study of demons; it is simply the study of what people from certain countries or cities call themselves. Or, put simply in Texas lingo: What do all y´all up there in Amarillo call yourselves? Amarilloans or Amarillians?

There are general rules for demonyms, but nothing that cannot be broken for phonetic aesthetics — for what sounds good.

For instance, cities or towns ending in "s" or "n" generally get an "-ites" ending. This is a biblical tradition carried on from names like Canaanites, Jebusites, etc.

So folks in Dallas are Dallasites. People in Dumas, Texas, are Dumasites. People in Paris, Texas, are Parisites … Well, that is an unfortunate result. So people there have adopted the French custom and call themselves Parisians. Much better.

And this variation of form is true for all the Texas towns named for European cities. Folks from Naples, Texas, are Neapolitans. People living in Liverpool, Texas, are Liverpudlians. Moscow, Texas, has Muscovites. We also have an Oxford, Texas. Well, truthfully, Oxford, Texas, has died out. So the only Oxonians still there are in the cemetery.

We have many unusual, rather unpredictable demonyms in Texas. Ivanhoe folks could be Ivanhoers, but if you say it too fast it sounds indelicate. So Ivanhoans is preferred. Carthage? Carthaginians. Leander? Leanderthals. That one is the result of an important archaeological find near there.

What do you call people in Cactus? Cacti? Would that be right? That's the Latin plural. Maybe Cactusites. Sounds like something in a cave. Could be Cactusians, but that sounds like a sneeze. That one is tough. What about Cut and Shoot? They are Cut and Shooters. Rough crowd. Commerce, Texas, is also a challenge. Are they Commercials? Commercians? No, probably Commercites. The demonym for denizens of Waco is not Wackos. It is Wacoans.

Comfort is interesting. Are they Comforters? Actually, yes. Dime Box has Dime Boxers. Alice, a rugged blue-collar oil-services town, has a truly sophisticated demonym. They are Alicians. Love that.

Corpus Christi is made up of Corpus Christians. No better demonym for the rapture.

For places ending in "-o," just add "-an." Laredo? Laredoans. San Angelo? San Angeloans. El Paso? El Pasoans. Amarillo? Depends on whether you say Amarillo or Amarilla. George Strait sings "Amarillo by Morning." So I go with him. The demonym, therefore, must be Amarilloans, and the website Amarillo.com confirms this.

San Antonio, though, doesn't follow this rule. San Antonioans is phonetically awkward. So we throw out the rule and just go with what sounds better: San Antonians.

If you have an "-on" ending, then by custom add "-ian" to create the demonym. Houston; Houstonian. Sinton; Sintonian. Denton should be Dentonian, but many people there prefer Dentonite. I have even heard Dentite, but I think that is Seinfeldian.

Hamilton; Hamiltonian. Jefferson; Jeffersonian. Should get those towns together for a good political debate.

The citizens of Refugio, going by the Spanish meaning, could be Refugees. But the town name ends in an "o" and the "g" is pronounced as if it were "r" . . . so once again we have phonetic chaos. Refu(r)ioans? No, Refu(r)ians. Falfurrias, being a Lipan-Apache derivative, has a similar result: Falfurrians, or the Spanish version Falfurrianos.

People in Austin seem to prefer Austinites. But a case could be made for Austinians. There is a town in Australia called Darwin, and they are Darwinians, so Austinian would be fine by precedent. Austonian, though, cannot be the demonym. It is the adjective and describes styles associated with the city (and is also the name of a big luxury high-rise downtown where some well-heeled Austinites live). You can say, "I love Austonian architecture," for instance.

Anything ending in "ville" is simple: Brownsvillians. Pflugervillians.

For places ending in ¨burg¨ you just add "-er." I´m gonna make you hungry now: Edinburgers, Fredericksburgers, Rosenburgers. Seems like we should have a town in Texas named Whataburg, whose residents would then be Whataburgers. I might move there just to be one.

Comanche, you would think, would have Comanches, but as they are not of the tribe, they are Comancheans.

San Marcos, San Marcoans. Corsicana, Corsicanonites? No. Corsicanans.

Does Buda have Budists? I think they are Budans, but be sure to pronounce that first syllable to rhyme with PEW, not with BOO.

I suppose the folks in Martin could be Martians, but more likely Martinites.

Citizens of Marfa are Marfans. But if they were Marfalites, it would be good marketing.

People in Paradise are Paradisians.

Happy has Happians.

Wink has Winkers.

Vega, Texas, has Vegans.

And Victoria has Victorians.

We even have demonyms by regions. We have the Llano Estacadoans, we have the Big Benders, and we have the Panhandlers.

But no matter what we are by demonym, we are all collectively Texans. And that, to me, is about the best thing in the world a person can be.

MONIKERS AND MOTTOES

Sometimes a town's nickname is a matter of civic marketing; other times it's something that just kinda stuck. Often, a town has both kinds.

Huntsville's nickname is Prison City, for example, and sometimes Execution Capital of the World. You won't find either name on the Chamber of Commerce marquee, but they are well-known monikers for the town, home to the Huntsville Unit of the Texas State Penitentiary, which houses the state's execution chamber.

Austin used to be known as the City of the Violet Crown, then Bat City, or Hippie Haven, and more lately Live Music Capital of the World, where folks are exhorted to "Keep Austin Weird." The university town of Denton, variously monikered Little D or the Redbud Capital of Texas, is also known as Little Austin.

Pecos is the site of the "World's First Rodeo," but Mesquite is the Rodeo Capital of Texas. Bandera is the Cowboy Capital of Texas, while Fort Worth is Cowtown — strange that the cowboys and the cows are 300 miles apart. Fort Worth, also once known as Panther City, is widely touted as "Where the West Begins" and shares with Dallas the title of the Metroplex.

Midland and Odessa share the Petroplex as their nickname, but Odessa is also known as the Jackrabbit Roping Capital. That must be a lot like herding cats (although safer than the World's Largest Rattlesnake Roundup in Sweetwater). For sheer business macho, I like Midlothian: the Cement and Steel Capital of Texas. As a counterbalance, we have Happy, Texas, the Town Without a Frown.

Marfa has been "Leaving the Lights on for You for 120 Years." Alpine calls itself the Gateway to Big Bend. Brady is the True Heart of Texas, being the closest town to the state's geographical center. Eagle Pass on the border is "Where Yee-Ha Meets Olé." And Fort Davis is "Where the Stars Come Out to Play." Corpus Christi is the Shining City by the Sea, while Brownsville is "On the Border by the Sea."

Burnet and Llano share the title of Bluebonnet Capital of Texas. More memorable is the slogan coined in response to those misinformed folks who say "Bur-NETTE": "It's BURN-it, durn it; can't you learn it?"

Mexia, which the locals pronounce "Muh-HAY-uh," is gentler with the pronunciation-challenged. There they say, "Mexia is a great place no matter how you pronounce it."

Commerce is the Bois d'Arc Capital of Texas, so named for the trees whose wood was prized by Indians for making bows. It's pronounced BOW-dark — you know, the trees with those grapefruit-sized wrinkly chartreuse fruits commonly called hedge apples or horse apples that nobody has ever been able to figure out a use for but that inspired the tree's other common name, Osage orange.

McCarney is the Wind Energy Capital of Texas. Might better go to Austin when the Legislature is in session.

We have several towns that claim to be the Watermelon Capital, of either Texas or the world: Naples, Weatherford, Hempstead, Dilley, Luling. But Dilley is the only one with a watermelon monument, and Luling (home of the venerable annual Watermelon Thump) has a watermelon water tower, so we'll let them fight it out for the win. Besides, Weatherford also claims to be the Peach Capital of Texas and the Cutting Horse Capital of Texas. So let's not get greedy there, Weatherford.

Getting a bit more specific, Knox City is the Seedless Watermelon Capital of Texas, officially designated by the Texas Legislature because the seedless watermelon was nurtured from an idea into a worldwide phenomenon right there on a nearby farm. Probably much cleaner sidewalks In Knox City than in those other watermelon capitals.

We have lots of other food capitals — Lockhart for barbecue, Elgin for sausage, Mauriceville for crawfish, Terlingua for chili, and Friona is the cheeseburger capital. Corsicana, thanks to the legitimately world-famous Collin Street Bakery, is the Fruitcake Capital of the World. Athens is the Black-Eyed Pea Capital. I bet they do some good business New Year's Day.

And after all that food you may want to go to Hereford, "The Town Without a Toothache."

El Paso is the Sun City, or El Chuco (from the Mexican-American Pachuco culture that is said to have originated there). Waco is the Buckle of the Bible Belt. Smithville is the Heart of the Megalopolis, quite a big name for a town of some three thousand.

Nacogdoches bills itself as the oldest town in Texas, but so does San Augustine.

Galveston is Oleander City, Tyler is the Rose Capital of the World and Georgetown the Red Poppy Capital, but San Angelo is the End of the Rainbow.

I think I'd like to go there. Sounds peaceful.

TEXAS BABY NAMES

If you watch old Westerns about Texas, you hear names like Tex, Laredo, Rio, Hondo, Amarillo. You hear dialogue like this: "Tex, you seen Rio around? Nope, but I saw Amarillo riding off to look for Laredo, and you know wherever Laredo is, Rio's close by."

You can't tell whether they are talking about people or places.

In modern Texas, you don't often meet people called Hondo and Laredo anymore.

Texas babies are now more likely to be named for bigger Texas cities: Dallas, Houston, Austin.

In fact, go into any first-grade classroom and you can hear a quick tour of the state from the teacher: "Austin, you and Dallas come up here and help Houston plant these bluebonnets."

It's fascinating that the original cities took the last names of the founders and now kids get those last names as first names.

Some smaller towns have gotten in on the trend. We seemed to have moved farther east from the Old West days. Tyler is quite popular. Crockett, too. And so is Beaumont. Beaumont always sounds very Texan to me, but it also sounds like someone who could be a character in a Jane Austen novel: "My dear Miss Emma, I'd like the honor of introducing you to Mr. Beaumont Farnsworth."

Twenty years ago, the most popular baby names for boys in Texas were Michael, Christopher and Joshua. Dominating the last 10 years have been José, Jacob and Daniel, though lately Jayden, Noah and Ethan have been trending strong.

The most popular Texas baby names for girls 20 years ago were Ashley, Jessica and Amanda. For the last decade, the top baby names for girls in the state have been Sophia, Isabella and Emily, followed very closely by Emma and Mia.

If you are looking for Hispanic names, there are plenty of great suggestions in Texas cities and towns. Antonio, of course; Goliad, which is almost an anagram for Hidalgo. And there is Hidalgo itself, also a Texas town. Refugio might be an option, though it is mostly pronounced "Refurio" by people who live there. Don't know where that extra "r" comes from. Mercedes would be a beautiful option. Roma would be nice . . . capital of Italy, too.

Actually, If anyone would like to name their new baby after great capitals of the world AND a Texas town, they have several options for such a two-for-one deal. We have 'em all — Paris, London, Moscow, Athens, Edinburgh, Stockholm, Berlin . . . well, New Berlin, but close enough.

And if you want something different from everybody else, cities and towns that are rarely chosen might be worth considering for your new Texas baby name:

Wichita after Wichita Falls; good for boy or girl. Wichita Jones. Falfurrias you never hear. Falfurrias Rodriguez. Waco? Waco Williams? Abilene, boy or girl. Never hear Corpus used. Corpus Roca would be good for a future weightlifter. Alpine would work for a boy or a girl. Sherman. Victoria. Lubbock for a boy. Lubbock Anderson. And let's not forget counties. I named one of my sons for Dawson County. Named him Dawson, not County, that is. If I ever have another boy, I'll name him after Falcon Dam and just call him Dam. Dam Strong.

TALKIN' ABOUT TEXAS WEATHER

When Admiral Perry arrived at the North Pole, according to Texas legend, he said, "Must be a cold day in Amarillo!" He was referring, of course, to the old Texas saying that there is nothing between Amarillo and the North Pole but a barbed-wire fence.

Amarillo and the Panhandle are not just famous for arctic fronts and blue northers. They are well known for wind in general. Chicago is not really the king of windy cities; Amarillo is. The Weather Channel says that Amarillo is the windiest city in America.

In fact, four of the 10 windiest cities in America are in Texas — Amarillo,

Photo by Carol M. Highsmith, Lyda Hill Texas Collection

Lubbock, Abilene and Corpus Christi. Windy weather is why Texas is by far No. 1 one in wind energy, producing more than twice as much as No. 2, Iowa.

Another common saying in Texas is this: "If you don't like the weather, just wait a minute." We are a region that can have the heater on in the morning and the air conditioner on at noon, only to turn the heater back on at night. In weather, we are bipolar. I like this post that's floating around the net these days: "Mother Nature: You can't squeeze all the weather in the world into one week. Texas: Hold my beer."

And it's not uncommon to see signs in Texas during the summer that say: "Satan called. He wants his weather back."

Here's another Texas expression I love: "It's hotter than a fur coat in Marfa." See if you can't work that one into conversation someday soon.

Despite the persistence of the claim that you can fry an egg on the sidewalk, it is never actually hot enough to fry an egg on the sidewalk. It does get hot enough to bake cookies on the dash, though, and I'd much rather have dashboard cookies than sidewalk eggs, anyway.

My brother Redneck Dave used to be annoyed that Freer often reported the highest summertime temperature in the state. He felt they were giving themselves an unfair advantage.

"I know for a fact that they keep their town thermometer in an oilfield pipe yard," he would say. "That ain't right."

Much of Texas is known for being dry. Dry as a bone, they often say. A West Texas rancher once told me, "God ain't much of a rainer out here, but he was mighty generous with the stars."

And they have sandstorms in West Texas so intense that sand drifts are left behind. In some years they have to shovel snow in the winter and sand in the summer. I bet sometimes they get to do this on the same day.

Farmers I knew as a kid would say that south Texas was so hot and dry that "the trees were whistling for the dogs." Gotta love farmers. Humor as dry as the land.

Eventually, though, droughts are broken and the rain comes. Then we have "gullywashers and toad-stranglers." Or old-timers might say, "It's raining so hard the animals are startin' to pair up." The legendary Galveston meteorologist Isaac Cline got it right when he said: "Texas is a land of eternal drought interrupted occasionally by biblical floods."

Houston is known not so much for rain or drought, but for humidity. It is a giant sauna much of the year. I doubt Houston would be the economic powerhouse it is if it weren't for air-conditioning. In 1900, there were fewer than 50,000 Houstonians. It won't be too long now before there will be 7 million people in the greater Houston area. What happened in the last century? The invention and perfection of air-conditioning. Coincidence? I think not.

Somewhere in Houston they should have a big statue of Willis Carrier, 100 feet tall, maybe right off the Gulf Freeway. Willis would reside comfortably inside a huge glass display case, which would be air-conditioned, of course.

In Texas we define ideal weather as Chamber of Commerce weather. That may not be unique to Texas, but it is a common expression here. Honestly, though, that kind of weather is rare. Most of the time, when I visit a Texas town for the first time people tell me, "The weather isn't usually like this." But from my experience it is.

SIZE MATTERS: BIG STUFF

TEXAS USED TO BE BIGGER

Texans have a saying: "Driving across Texas isn't a trip; it's a damn career."

Texas is big, no doubt about that. But it used to be a lot bigger. About a fourth bigger.

When Texas joined the United States in 1845, Texas' borders (and shape) were quite different.

The northern boundary of Texas in those days stretched all the way up into what is today southern Wyoming. It´s true. In those days, the northern-most town in Texas was not Dalhart, it was Rawlins. You think it´s a long way from Brownsville to Dalhart now — at 860 miles — try 1400 miles to Raw-lins. In 1845 a trip like that would have been measured in seasons, not days: "We'll leave in early spring and get there before winter sets in."

Texas used to have a panhandle for the Panhandle (which wasn't exactly a panhandle then because it was much wider, taking up half of what's now New Mexico). The Panhandle's panhandle passed through prime Colorado Rock-ies real estate (including Vail) into Wyoming. They called that the stovepipe because that is what it looked like: a long skinny stovepipe, jutting northward and just slightly westward above Texas' "roof" a bit north of the present Colo-rado and Kansas state lines. You can still find vestiges of Texas up there in that part of Wyoming; there is a creek up there in that region named Texas Creek.

Texas used to include what is today the panhandle of Oklahoma. That area now comprises three counties — Cimarron, Beaver and Texas. So some Oklahomans still live in Texas — Texas County, anyway.

The southwestern tip of Kansas was also part of Texas. Dodge City was in Texas. Glad to know that, since *Gunsmoke* always seemed like a Texas series. The character of Marshal Matt Dillon was born in San Antonio, we know. His father was a Texas Ranger. It's all coming together.

New Mexico used to be about half its current size because Santa Fe and Taos and all the eastern part of the state was Texas. Texas was so big in 1845 that if you had put a hinge on the northernmost part and flipped it north-ward, Brownsville would have been in Northern Canada next to Hudson Bay. Don´t think those Brownsvillians would have liked trading the tropics for the tundra, but that would have been the result. If you had flipped Texas southward, the people of Rawlins would have been in Peru. The east-west boundaries would have been closer to what they are today. Still, flip Texas eastward and you would have El Pasoans trading their margaritas for mint juleps in Georgia. Flip it westward and the Beaumontians would be hanging ten with California surfer dudes.

So what happened to all our land? The U.S. government bought it in 1850. For $10 million they bought our claims to Wyoming, Colorado, New Mexico, Kansas and Oklahoma. It came to 6.7 cents an acre. Seems like we sold out cheap, but we desperately needed the money then. And remember that $10 million in 1850 is $300 million in today's dollars, which is almost enough to buy a nice vacation home in Vail.

But, as I said, we really needed the money. We had a state to build, and the only true assets we had in those days were land — and a tough, hardened people of unbreakable spirits. So we sold the land and paid off debts and got a much more appealing shape to the state, a shape that fits nicely on T-shirts.

And even thus diminished, we are nonetheless no slouch of a state, especially by car. We still measure distance in time. We still feel like we are crossing an enormous frontier when driving I-10 through West Texas or I-69 to the southern border. And this old Texas saying is still valid: "The sun has riz; the sun has set; and here I is in Texas yet."

TEXAS VS. ALASKA

There's a popular bumper sticker up there in Alaska that says, "Pissing Off Texans Since 1959."

The allusion is, of course, to the fact that when Alaska became a state, Texas immediately got demoted to second place in the biggest-state contest.

Texans were fond of pointing out that if we melted all the ice and snow up there Texas would still be bigger.

We are certainly bigger in population — 40 times bigger. But Alaska, from a woman's perspective, has an attractive ratio of men to women: 6 to 4, some say. A female friend from Texas who lived up there a while told me that the "odds are good but the goods are odd." But I have to be careful here. Alaskans are also fond of taunting Texas by saying, "Don't get us mad or we'll split in two and make you the third-largest state."

There's no doubt that Alaska is geographically more than twice the size of Texas, but we do still own the bragging rights on many fronts.

After all, Texas reigned as the biggest state in the union for 104 years. Alaska has a long way to go to take that title from us, about 50 years yet.

Second thing. You know that famous pipeline they have up there. Guess who built it. Texans did. And Okies, too. There are no exact figures, but we have proof in Alaskan folklore. An Alaskan saying back when the pipeline was being built was this: "Happiness is 10,000 Okies pickin' up a Texan under each arm and headin' south." Don't know why they would have that attitude. We were just making 'em rich.

Third thing. Despite Alaska's fame for oil, Texas is still a much larger producer of oil and gas and has far greater reserves. Texas remains No. 1 in oil production in the United States and would be the sixth-largest oil country in the world if she were on her own. They don't call us Saudi Texas for nothing. We have three times as much oil as Alaska, and 10 times as much natural gas.

Final thing, and a kind of slam-dunk fact: Alaska would not be a state if Texas had not made her one. It's true. Alaska's bid for statehood had languished for years back in the '40s and '50s. The proposal had been going nowhere until Texans Lyndon Johnson, one of the U.S. Senate's most powerful members, and Sam Rayburn, speaker of the House, threw their weight behind Alaska's statehood ambitions. That was the tipping point. Once those two got behind it, Alaska was fast-tracked to statehood. You might say Texas was big enough to let Alaska be bigger.

The Texas-Alaska rivalry is mostly a faux feud. We are deeply connected. Hell, you can choose from 40 flights a day to go from Houston to Anchorage. There is probably no better state friendship than ours, because we are kindred states — we've both had frontier histories, oil booms and busts, and we are made of fiercely independent peoples who insist on shaping their own destinies. But if global warming continues, we may one day see if Alaska, under all that ice and snow, is really bigger than Texas.

ONE TEXAN IN THE GLOBAL VILLAGE

There is an unusual map of the world that was once a popular poster. You still see it around, because it is a map that makes you see the world in new ways. This map reduces the world's 7.3 billion people to a village of just 100 people. It keeps all the ratios the same, so we can get a look at the world in miniature.

So on this map you will see that there are 60 Asians in the world — that's counting China and Japan and India and Eastern Russia. More than half of the world lives in Asia.

Europe has 11 people. Africa has a few more — 16 — but a lot more room. If you add all of the Americas together, from the North Pole all the way down to Tierra del Fuego in Argentina, you get 14 people.

The United States accounts for only five people. And Texas? Texas has one person in this village. Imagine. Out of the entire population of this vast planet, only one gets the honor, the rare pleasure, of being a Texan.

Reminds me of another map observation from Bob Wheeler, author of *Forged of a Hotter Fire*. I like to mention Wheeler's book whenever I can because his work floats around the internet with his name divorced from it. He gets no credit. The quotation below is often credited to Bum Phillips — a great lover of Texas for sure, but he did not write *Forged of a Hotter Fire*; Bob Wheeler did.

Here is what Wheeler has to say in his marvelous little Tex-centric book:

"Look at Texas for me for just a second. That picture with the Panhandle and the Gulf Coast and the Red River and the Rio Grande is as much a part of you as anything ever will be. As soon as anyone anywhere in the world looks at it they know what it is. It's Texas. Take any kid off the street in Japan and draw him a picture of Texas in the dirt and he'll know what it is."

Wheeler said he thought that "most everyone everywhere would like, just once, to be a real Texan — to ride a horse or drive a pickup." Perhaps they long to drive off to the freedom of vast blue skies to horizons unknown. Wheeler believed that everyone, deep down, had a longing for something that might be called Texas. Might well be so.

THE SHAMROCK HOTEL

See if you recognize this voice:

My well came in, Bick.

. . . Everybody thought I had a duster? Y'all thought ole Spindletop and ole Burk Burnett was all the oil there was, didn't you?

That's James Dean in the movie *Giant*, adapted from Edna Ferber's potboiler novel. Dean is telling the cattle-baron Benedict family, headed by Rock Hudson and Elizabeth Taylor as Bick and Leslie Benedict, that he has struck oil. And not only that: It's payback time.

I'm rich, Bick. I'm a rich'un . . . I'm a rich boy. Me, I'm gonna have more money'n you ever THOUGHT you could have — you and all the rest of you stinkin' sons of Benedicts.

James Dean was playing Jett Rink, a hard-drinkin', hard-brawlin', tough-talkin' uncultured Texas wildcatter who struck it rich on the little sliver of land left to him by Bick's older sister Luz. But everybody in Texas knew that he was really playing Glen McCarthy, a Beaumont-born Houston wildcatter, who struck it rich in a similar way — cover-of-*Time* rich. In the movie, the fictional Jett Rink spent millions of dollars building the Emperador, the biggest hotel in Texas. The real-life McCarthy did the same. But he called his hotel the Shamrock.

The Shamrock, nicknamed the Houston Riviera, was the grandest hotel in Texas when it was built. It was touted as being the biggest hotel built in the United States in the post-war era up to that point and the largest hotel, old or new, outside of New York or L.A. when it was finished in 1949. It was 20 stories tall, counting the two-story emerald *SHAMROCK HOTEL* sign on top. It cost upwards of $22 million, which would translate to $250 million today. It had an outdoor swimming pool that McCarthy claimed as the biggest on the planet — so large that people could water-ski in it, and did, as staged publicity stunts. It had 1100 rooms, all air-conditioned, and a TV and radio in every room.

In 1949, McCarthy wanted to have a grand opening for his monolithic hotel. He wanted Hollywood stars. He was told that the only way Hollywood would come was if there was a movie opening to attend. But no big studio would launch a film in Texas. So he decided to fund his own Hollywood movie, which would allow him to have the movie debut and hotel grand opening at the same time. Which he did: *The Green Promise,* starring Walter Brennan and Natalie Wood. And Hollywood came. McCarthy's new friend Howard Hughes flew McCarthy into Houston with him from L.A. McCarthy chartered a party train to brought in hundreds of stars for the St. Patrick's Day opening.

The evening was regarded as one of the most prestigious events in Houston social history. And it likely remains so. Ginger Rogers was there. So was Errol Flynn. It was broadcast live on national radio by NBC and hosted by the World War II pinup heroine Dorothy Lamour.

Heavyweight architects, Frank Lloyd Wright among them, weren't impressed with the Shamrock's 63 shades of Irish green, lobbing various colorfully caustic remarks its way. But many loved the Shamrock for its sheer size, its over-the-top art-deco style, the Emerald Nightclub where Sinatra sang, the Cork Club up top overlooking Houston and the hotel's overall grand devotion to the Irish theme.

It was sold in to Conrad Hilton in 1955 and was known as the Shamrock Hilton until it was demolished in 1987. Today Texas A&M Health Sciences Center sits on the site. I think McCarthy might like that. He was, after all, an Aggie.

THE SCARIEST BRIDGE IN TEXAS

There's more than one Texas bridge that can be especially troubling for those with gephyrophobia — fear of bridges.

The Pecos railroad bridge can certainly give you the willies from the right perspective. The Corpus Christi Harbor Bridge can give you pause if the outer bands of a tropical storm should arrive when you're up on top. Some of those

The Rainbow Bridge over the Neches River.

five-stack interchanges in Dallas and Houston can cause a palpitation or two, but in my opinion, the scariest bridge in Texas is the Rainbow Bridge over the Neches River between Port Arthur and Orange, on Texas Highway 73.

It offers the triple threat: You can see it coming from a long way off. It has a steep ascent and descent. And it rises frighteningly high over water. Those are the things gephyrophobics most dread.

The Rainbow Bridge is scary enough today, with its two lanes of one-way southbound traffic (the nearby Veterans' Memorial Bridge, built in 1991, now handles the northbound traffic). But it used to be much worse. For many decades, drivers had to put up with two thin lanes carrying cars and 18-wheelers in both directions. As you arrived near the top of the bridge, all you could see was sky in the daytime and the stars at night. You just had to have faith that the pavement would be there waiting for you when you passed over the hump. It was enough to make some folks take a 30-mile detour to avoid the stress.

Seems odd that a bridge with such a nice name could cause such fear. Local driver's ed teachers often made students drive over that bridge on their first day of class. They believed that the best way to conquer a fear was to face it — head on — right away.

When it was completed in 1938, it was the tallest in Texas and among the tallest in America, at essentially 20 stories high. Originally, it was called the Neches River Bridge or the Port Arthur-Orange Bridge.

I used to believe that the Rainbow Bridge name came from Norse mythology, wherein the rainbow bridge called *Biforst* connects heaven and earth. But no. In 1957 the North Port Arthur Lions Club had a naming contest, and 6-year-old Christy McClintock submitted the winning entry. She said the bridge looked like a mechanical rainbow. And it does indeed. If you ever are there towards sunset and see it illuminated in those pink hues of the evening, it does look like a steel rainbow. Christy got a $50 savings bond as her prize. Doesn't sound like much today, but in 1957 you could have bought 200 Whataburgers with it.

Why was the bridge built so tall, with 177 feet of vertical clearance, in that delta region? Well, there was an important ship channel there, and they wanted the tallest ship in the Navy at the time, the USS Patoka, to be able to pass easily beneath it, pulling a dirigible.

The Rainbow Bridge was more than an engineering marvel. It was also a magnet for teenagers in the night, when local high school kids used to climb up into the catwalks. One of those students, legend has it, used to sit up there high above the moonlit waters of the Neches River and sing in her passionately raw style. I'm sure you've heard of her. Janis Joplin? Her biographer, Myra Friedman, has said that she would sing up there under the great Texas sky and "scorch the stars." But that's a whole 'nother story. I'm just giving you the abridged version. (That pun is free.)

The tallest ship in the Navy never did sail beneath the Rainbow Bridge. Seems a shame. Somewhat like a bride having planned a perfect wedding, and then the groom never showed.

AUSTIN'S MOONLIGHT TOWERS

The first time I heard the term "Moontower," I heard it from Matthew McConaughey. He didn't say it to me personally. He said it to a carload of teenagers in Richard Linklater's movie *Dazed and Confused.*

There was a "party at the Moontower," he told them. Next thing you see are dozens of kids sharing a keg of brew and sharing their angst beneath, and on top of, a 165-foot tower.

These towers with the romantic name, I've since learned, are emblematic to Austin. There were originally 31 of them, but now only 17 Moonlight Towers, as they are more properly called, remain in service. We know the switch was flipped to illuminate all 31 towers, Austin's first public street-lighting system, on May 3, 1895. A number of other forward-thinking cities around the country had already installed electric light towers to provide improved lighting to their streets and neighborhoods at night. Today, Austin is the only place these towers are still standing today.

But there are two narratives about their origin, the more commonly repeated one being that Austin purchased them, secondhand, from the city of

Detroit — which was the first major city to install a system of towers — in 1894.

Other historians, however, maintain that they were purchased new from Indiana's Fort Wayne Electric Co., which assembled them on-site. One account reports that, along with a cash payment of $70,000 for the towers, the city was to throw in a narrow-gauge railroad it had used to transport materials to the newly constructed Austin Dam on the Colorado River, which was to provide electricity to power the towers via dynamos installed by the Indiana company. (The film documentary *Last of the Moonlight Towers* notes that the trade never took place; the city instead sold the railroad and used the proceeds to complete the payment.)

Photo by Carol M. Highsmith, Lyda Hill Collection

One of the 17 Moonlight Towers that still stand today in Austin.

The documentary touches on both origin stories, but co-producer Jeffrey Kerr seems to lean toward the purchased-new story. Kerr, who has published three books about Austin history, believes the confusion may have arisen from the fact that Detroit's towers were made by the same company as Austin's. Indeed, historical photographs of the Detroit towers show a strong resemblance to Austin's models.

They were big: 150 feet tall (165 feet tall once erected on their bases), resembling skinny oil derricks, but with their triangular scaffolding mounted on a single pipe at the base and stabilized by guy wires. And heavy. Made of cast iron. And bright — housing six carbon arc lights at their peak, like stationary searchlights, that lit up the ground below brighter than a full moon could. The city fathers believed they would reduce crime and make the nighttime city safer for walking, and more enjoyable.

The lights were installed across the entire city, in rich and poor neighborhoods alike (the first one was erected in the tony neighborhood of Hyde Park, which was then being developed as Austin's first suburb). They produced a light so bright that you could read your watch by them a quarter-mile away.

Each tower lit about half a square mile. It was a beautiful notion — to use the moon as your model for lighting the night. The idea was to create mini-moons and lift them high above the city to give the effect of an eternal full moon. How magical it sounded.

But the arc lighting was so bright that it had to be mounted high above the ground, and situating the lights atop 16-story towers, far above trees and buildings, resulted in broad, stark shadows that plunged some homes into darkness and made it more difficult to see when moving from light to dark. In times of fog the lights lit up the air above the fog and permeated the ground cloud with an eerie blue light that frightened people. Some believe that the lights were in fact purchased because of a serial killer, the Servant Girl Annihilator, who had terrorized Austin a decade earlier, though *Last of the Moonlight Towers'* Kerr and his co-producer Ray Spivey doubt that was a major impetus.

Plenty of folks found all this night lighting just unnatural. If God had wanted us to have light all the time, they reasoned, he wouldn't have made night. Some feared that the Moonlight Tower lights would make the grass grow 24 hours a day so that they would have to mow more often. Some worried that the lights would keep people up all night and make Austin's work force sleepy, tired and cranky. Others believed that the chickens wouldn't roost and egg production would drop off. Dogs would never stop barking.

Since then, of course, more modern types of bulbs have replaced the original arc lamps. Today, about half the original Moonlight Towers still stand, having undergone a major restoration beginning in 1993 and finished in time for their centennial. In 2014, the city approved a fund of $3.9 million to restore and maintain them. All 17 are working. And Austin is the only city in the world where these structures still are still part of the electric night-lighting grid. Amazing, really.

THE VAST LAND: TALES OF TEXAS PAST

CABEZA DE VACA

The first European to waltz across Texas — OK, waltz is the wrong word; just tipping my hat to Ernest Tubb there. The first European to walk across Texas was Cabeza de Vaca. And he did at least part of it, we are told, barefoot and at least partially naked.

His full name was Álvar Núñez Cabeza de Vaca. "Álvar" is said to mean *guardian* or *truth-speaker*. Turns out that he could have been considered something close to a guardian — or at least an advocate — for the indigenous peoples of the Americas, given the general sympathy he was to display toward them as opposed to the general contempt in which they were held from the very beginning by most Europeans. In Spain, many sources agree, he advocated for better treatment of the natives by the invading Spaniards.

Cabeza de Vaca started his adventures in the New World as treasurer of a Spanish naval expedition that left Spain in 1527 with the mission of exploring and colonizing Florida. About 300 of the Spaniards, with 40 horses, came ashore near present-day Tampa Bay in the spring of 1528 with the mission of exploring northward and then became separated from the expedition's ships. Within a few months, fighting Indian attacks and starvation, the 250 or so who were left had made their way to the Florida peninsula, where they managed to build five large rafts in order to escape into the Gulf of Mexico. They used their horses for food and their clothes for sails. They hugged the coastline and made it to the mouth of the Mississippi River, which pushed them out to sea, where they were separated by currents and storms. Many died from drinking seawater in desperation. Many fell overboard and drowned.

Most of the rafts eventually made landfall on the coast of what is now Texas, from Galveston Island to Matagorda Bay. The raft captained by Cabeza de Vaca washed up on an island near Galveston (probably what is now Follet's Island or San Luis Island, just southwest of Galveston Island), along with another raft, bearing from 50 to 90 survivors — reports vary — in total. They tried to repair their rafts, but the crafts were washed away, leaving the survivors without clothes, food or gear.

Native Indians on the island rescued the castaways and fed them as best they could, but many of the men died of malnutrition and illness. Many of the Indians died too, likely from European viruses that de Vaca's group carried. Those who survived from the Spanish expedition were at the mercy of the Coahuiltecan Indians, being forced to dig for edible roots, gather firewood and keep fires going all night to ward off the swarms of mosquitoes. They were often beaten. It is not surprising that they named the island where they had made landfall *Isla de Malhado* — Isle of Misfortune.

Cabeza de Vaca, however, eventually managed to make his way to the mainland. While he was gone, 12 of the surviving men left and walked on down the coast, only to die of starvation and attacks by less friendly Indians. Only two Spaniards and one African slave remained on the island.

Meanwhile, on the mainland, de Vaca had become a trader, carrying trade goods inland during the summer and receiving food in return for his ministrations to ailing Indians, who believed he had healing power. But eventually he reunited with his surviving compatriots on the coast, where they remained at the mercy of the Karankawas.

They were stuck in this hellish situation for several years. Despite the tribulations they endured, a tiny hope sustained them: Cortez was only 1,000 miles away down in Mexico. Maybe they could reach him. Eventually, they were able to make their escape and strike out towards Mexico.

They headed southwest, probably following the coastal route that is today Texas State Highway 35. They had escaped with virtually no clothes or shoes. They had to navigate an increasingly brutal terrain of mesquite thickets and cactus and sharp coastal grasses. They ate pecans, prickly pear fruit, prickly pear pads and mesquite beans. "It was an "extreme tale of survival: four naked men at the mercy of the natural elements, facing an extraordinary array of native societies," historian Andres Resendez wrote in his book *A Land So Strange: The Epic Journey of Cabeza de Vaca.*

The exact route of their journey will never be known, but by most accounts they turned temporarily westward as they approached Baffin Bay to avoid the treacherous desert-like sands that dominated the land south of there, between the bay and the Rio Grande.

Despite the difficulties of their journey, Cabeza de Vaca still marveled at the beauty of the coastal plains of Texas. He saw buffalo, which he called huge cows, and even tasted the meat once or twice, meat the natives gave him. He declared it better than European beef. He later recalled: "All over the land there are vast and handsome pastures with good grass for cattle, and it strikes me that the soil would be very fertile were the country inhabited and improved by reasoning people."

His speculation could be said to have foreshadowed the great cattle ranches such as the King Ranch that would flourish 300 years later. Cabeza de Vaca himself would later advocate colonizing the area through peaceful coexistence and cooperative colonization with the Indians.

One thing the castaways did have going for them is that they became known as healers — de Vaca, in particular. They were called "the Children of the Sun" by some Indians. Indians began flocking to them to be healed, and they did the best they could, blowing gently on their patients' bodies and making the sign of the cross over them. Sometimes they recited rosaries, which made them all the more mystical, I'm sure.

Fortunately, a number of the people they treated reported feeling better. So their reputation preceded them, and many of the tribes they encountered on their journey greeted them as holy men and demigods. Cabeza de Vaca himself scoffed at their purported healing powers, but in time he believed that God was working through them to save them. Why else would they be the last survivors of some three hundred? They must be blessed.

Cabeza de Vaca and friends trekked west and then southwest, possibly through the site of present-day Falfurrias and on to the site of Roma, where they crossed the Rio Grande. The route they took is much debated. Some say they went westerly toward Laredo or Eagle Pass. But we know for sure that they eventually turned northwest in Mexico, tramped up to the Big Bend region and then turned ever westward.

They walked all the way to what is believed to have been the Gulf of California in northwestern Mexico. They finally encountered some of their own countrymen, in Mexico to capture slaves, near what is now Culiacan. The Spanish soldiers were shocked by de Vaca's appearance: Hair down to his waist. Beard down to his chest. Hardly clothed. The castaways, after nearly a decade of travail, were saved. In 1536, almost a decade after they left Spain, they made it to Mexico City; eventually, de Vaca would return to Spain.

Cabeza de Vaca was the first European to get a good look at the magnificence of Texas and to leave behind a record of what it could become. He was Texas' first tourist, and, through his observations of and writings about the natives, its first ethnologist. He wrote Texas' first travel guide, you might say. And, despite the suffering he endured there, he gave Texas a five-star review for its possibilities.

FOR FURTHER READING: Chronicle of the Narvaez Expedition, *by Álvar Núñez Cabeza de Vaca;* A Land So Strange: The Epic Journey of Cabeza de Vaca, *by Andres Resendez.*

LAND RUSH

The most expensive ranch in Texas, when this book was going to press, was T. Boone Pickens' Mesa Vista Ranch in the Texas Panhandle. It was offered at the bargain-basement price of $250 million. That's right at 65,000 acres, including 25 miles of frontage on the Canadian River. Comes to only $3846 an acre, but for a cash deal I'm sure Boone might let you have it for just $3800 an acre or so. The ranch has its own airport, so you could just fly your cash right to him and close the deal.

I've got to say that's a far cry from the prices prospective Texans were paying for land in Stephen F. Austin's day.

Back in 1821, Stephen F. Austin was charging 12 1/2 cents an acre for a league of land, which was 4428 acres. This was by way of a venture Austin's father Moses had cooked up to establish an American colony in Spanish Texas, attracting Catholic settlers from Louisiana. Moses Austin, unfortunately, had died shortly after obtaining permission from the Spanish governor for a land grant to establish a settlement. On his deathbed, Moses exhorted his wife to "tell dear Stephen that it is his dieing fathers last request to prosecute the enterprise he had Commenced." So Austin dutifully traveled to Texas to find auspicious sites for settlements on the Brazos and Colorado rivers and then advertise them to prospective colonists.

His land deals changed several times due to political shifts from the Spanish and then Mexican powers that were, but at one point he was offering two deals, 4428 acres (a league) for raising stock and 177 acres (a labor) for raising crops. So you can imagine that many blacksmiths and woodcutters became farmers and ranchers right quick. And that's not all. Married men got far more land than single ones. So there was a stampede up the church aisles as single farmers rushed to become married ranchers. Imagine, you walk down the aisle with nothing and come out with almost 4500 acres. Compare that to today, where you walk in with $30,000 and walk out broke.

That was quite a deal Austin offered: 12 1/2 cents an acre (and mostly on credit) at a time when land in the United States was 10 times more than that. Someone later pointed out, "Land in Texas was what gold was to the gold rush."

A league of land for $550. Even adjusted for today's dollars it would be only $12,000, and 4428 acres is a lot of land. (But you still wouldn't have a King Ranch. Even with all those acres you would still own less than half a percent of the King Ranch. By comparison, you wouldn't even have a ranchito. You would have a ranchitito, essentially a postage stamp by the King Ranch scale.)

In deep South Texas, the original land grants of 4500 acres sold for even less: sometimes as little as the filing fee of $50 and other times for 10 cents an acre, with payments not starting until the fourth year of the seven-year term, to give you the chance to work the land and have it help pay for itself.

What I need is a good time machine. I wish I could go back to see my great-grandfather when he lived in East Texas. I could say to him, "Great-Gramps, here's $1,000. I want you to go over to Beaumont and find a little hill known around there as Spindletop. Buy that hill and the 4,000 acres that surrounds it. Here's another thousand for mineral rights. Drill for oil there. Live well. Leave it all in a trust to be shared by any of your descendants who are 6-foot-5 or more, blue-eyed and work in radio.

If only rebooting your life were that easy!

THE WILD HORSE DESERT

He was almost 24 years old and riding his horse south of Corpus Christi in the vicinity of what would one day be called the King Ranch.

But there wouldn't be a ranch there for another couple of decades.

In some ways it was a spooky place, ghostly. You would see horse tracks everywhere, but no people. Well-worn trails might have made it seem thickly inhabited, but the population was merely equestrian.

It was believed that these horses were the descendants of the steeds Cortez had brought over to conquer the Aztecs. Some of them had escaped, migrated north and bred freely in their new habitat. Because of them, this region would become known as the Wild Horse Desert by some, including Texana writer Brian Robertson, who would use the name as the title of his book on South Texas.

Our young man, a second lieutenant three years out of West Point, was riding with a regiment of soldiers under the command of Gen. Zachary Taylor. It was 1846. Texas had recently been annexed by the United States and Taylor was leading an "Army of Observation" under orders to establish Fort Texas on the Rio Grande to enforce that river's status as the southern border of the United States. Fort Texas would shortly become Fort Brown, the fort from which Brownsville, Texas, would take its name.

The young lieutenant loved horses. He had been an avid and skillful rider growing up in Georgetown, Ohio, and had excelled as a horseman at West Point. He was so impressed with the seemingly infinite herds of wild horses in South Texas that he made a note about them in his journal, later recalling in his memoir:

A few days out from Corpus Christi, the immense herd of wild horses that ranged at that time between the Nueces and the Rio Grande was seen directly in advance of the head of the column and but a few miles off. It was the very band from which the horse I was riding had been captured but a few weeks before.

The column was halted for a rest, and a number of officers, myself among them, rode out two or three miles to the right to see the extent of the herd. The country was a rolling prairie, and, from the higher ground, the vision was obstructed only by the earth's curvature. As far as the eye could reach to our right, the herd extended. To the left, it extended equally. There was no estimating the number of animals in it; I have no idea that they could all have been corralled in the State of Rhode Island, or Delaware, at one time. If they had been, they would have been so thick that the pasturage would have given out the first day.

Zachary Taylor was on the cusp of the Mexican-American War; his army would fight the first battle at Palo Alto on May 6, then cross into Mexico and head for Monterrey. His exploits in that war would help him become the 12th president of the United States.

His second lieutenant would also ascend to the presidency 20 years after him.

The young man on high ground surveying the vast scene of thousands of mustangs grazing before him would become the hero of many battles in the years ahead. He would ultimately win the Civil War and would become the youngest U.S. president for his time. His presidential memoir would be considered the best of all such memoirs, a runaway best seller in its day, a book Mark Twain would publish and call the most remarkable work of its kind since Caesar's *Commentaries*. It was titled *The Personal Memoirs of Ulysses S. Grant*, and it is that book that gives us this story.

FOR FURTHER READING: The Personal Memoirs of Ulysses S. Grant *has never gone out of print.*

THE TEXAS RANGERS AND THE COLT SIX-SHOOTER

God made some men big and some men small. Samuel Colt made equals of them all.

— Old frontier saying

The Colt six-shooter never would have been made had it not been for the Texas Rangers. That is a large claim, but I can prove it.

Before there was a Colt six-shooter, there was a Colt five-shooter, back in 1836. It was called the Colt Paterson, after the New Jersey city where it was made. This single-action .28-caliber pistol had a folding trigger and a reputation for being cantankerous and prone to break down in the field.

Samuel Colt couldn't sell it to much of anyone, except for a lucky sale to the Republic of Texas for use in the Texas Navy. When Texas joined the Union and its navy was retired, the surplus guns were appropriated by Capt.

John Coffee Hays for his Texas Rangers. The Rangers, for their part, found this five-shooter Colt invaluable in fighting the Comanches, the most feared warriors on the Texas plains.

The Comanches already had a rapid-fire weapon of their own. It was called a bow and arrow. A skilled warrior could pump four arrows into a Ranger before he could reload his old single-shot rifle. And the Comanches could do it from horseback, at a gallop. Colt's repeating revolver evened the playing field.

If there had been a MasterCard ad at that time, it might have gone like this:
Fastest quarter horse around: $100.
Top-of-the-line saddle: $40.
Two Colt revolvers: $60.
Going up against 40 Comanches with seven fellow Texas Rangers, equally equipped: Priceless.

Still, despite the Rangers' affection for his revolvers, Colt couldn't sell enough to keep his company afloat and eventually stopped manufacturing guns.

Then, in 1846, came the Mexican-American War. The Texas Rangers were making a name for themselves as part of the U.S. military effort in Mexico. Zachary Taylor preferred them as scouts; they were particularly skilled at mounted fighting; and they were ruthless against Mexican guerrillas. Among the most notorious was Samuel Walker.

Walker had used the Colt Paterson model during his former service as a Texas Ranger. After Taylor's forces had stormed Monterrey and secured the city, in 1846, there was a brief furlough, and Walker (no relation to the Chuck Norris TV character; see "Samuel Walker: The Real *Walker, Texas Ranger*," page 55) left Mexico and traveled back east. There, he contacted Samuel Colt with some suggestions for improvements for the previous Paterson pistol. He told Colt that the five-shooter should be made a six-shooter for better balance.

Thus the six-shooter was born. It was larger than the former model, and heavier, designed for mounted combat and meant to be carried in a saddle holster, not on a gunbelt. It was so heavy, in fact, that Colt was reputed to have said it would take a "Texan to shoot it."

This new pistol, produced in cooperation with Eli Whitney, of cotton-gin fame, was called the Walker Colt. Only 1100 were produced, with 1000 of those earmarked for the U.S. military, so they were rare and hard to come by. Every soldier wanted one. Every man in the West wanted one. A later version was called the Peacemaker, the gun that tamed the West.

As for Walker, he returned from Washington to rejoin the fighting in Mexico. When he was killed at the Battle of Huamantla in 1847, he was carrying the pair of Walker six-shooters he had just received as a gift from Colt.

FOR FURTHER READING: The Texas Rangers: A Century of Frontier Defense, *by Walter Prescott Webb.*

NOT WITHOUT THE CATTLE

Captain Leander McNelly and his special force of 30 Texas Rangers were pinned down in a row behind a line of brush on the Mexican side of the Rio Grande. They were surrounded by 400 Mexican soldiers and banditos. It was November 1875, near the Las Cuevas Ranch in northern Mexico. The embattled McNelly received word from the U.S. Cavalry, on the American side of the river, that he should retreat across the Rio Grande to U.S. soil. The cavalry unit would cover his return.

No, said Captain McNelly. Not without the cattle.

It had all started late the day before, when McNelly and his Rangers had come upon a U.S. Cavalry unit from Fort Ringgold. The cavalry had tracked a band of cattle thieves, herding their plunder on the hoof, to the Rio Grande but would not cross onto foreign soil. McNelly told them they should pursue while the trail was hot. The cavalry commander said they could not cross into another country's territory.

McNelly wasn't such a stickler about territory. His branch of the Texas Rangers had been created by the Texas governor as a Special Force to clean up the banditry and cattle thievery in the Nueces Strip north of the Rio Grande, and it was financed by the area's cattle ranchers. He was determined to get those cattle back.

The next morning, in the predawn darkness, McNelly and his Rangers moved stealthily on foot through the Mexican brush to where the cattle were believed to be corralled at the Las Cuevas Ranch. They had good fog cover as dawn broke. They advanced quickly to the ranch house and surprised a small band of armed men. There was a brief skirmish, and several of the Mexicans were killed. Only one problem: wrong house. It was merely a line camp, with no connection to the theft of the cattle.

Now, though, all the gunfire had alerted the men at the Las Cuevas ranch headquarters of the incursion. By the time the Rangers got near there, the local garrison of Mexican soldiers had been called out and the rangers faced a force of 400, many of them mounted.

Being on foot was now an advantage to the rangers, because they were camouflaged by the brush and the fog. They took out a good number of men and horses with rifle fire and then made a break for the river, two miles away. There they set up their defense positions. With the help of cover from a U.S. Calvary Gatling gun on the American side, they repulsed the Mexican attack. When the smoke cleared, counting the dead at the ranch, 80 Mexicans had been killed, including the soldiers' general, Juan Flores Salinas. The Rangers had suffered a few casualties, but none of them had been killed. Everything was eerily quiet.

The U.S. Cavalry commander now crossed the Rio Grande to give Mc-

Nelly a telegram containing orders from Col. J. H. Potter at Fort Brown: McNelly and his men were to retreat from Mexico, and the U.S. Cavalry was to give him no further aid whatsoever. This was communicated to the Mexican forces as well.

McNelly's answer was no. The commander was stunned. But McNelly confirmed his answer: He was not returning without the cattle.

The day passed at a standoff. The Mexicans reinforced their positions and McNelly refused to budge. Another telegram arrived for Col. Potter, this time conveying orders from the U.S. secretary of war in Washington: *Secretary of War [William W.] Belknap orders you to demand McNelly return at once to Texas. Do not support him in any manner.* McNelly was a Texas Ranger and did not believe he had to answer to the U.S. military. It had been not 15 years since he was leading troops *against* U.S. forces, in fact, as a captain in the Confederate Army whose unit had been one of the last to disband as the war ended.

When the orders were conveyed to him, he sent back a reply: *I shall remain in Mexico with my rangers and cross back at my discretion. Give my compliments to the Secretary of War and tell him and his United States soldiers to go to hell."*

Frustrated with the wait, McNelly warned the new Mexican commander that if he didn't get the cattle back within an hour, he would attack. The commander knew how lethal and reckless the Rangers could be, so he agreed to return the cattle the next day at the Camargo crossing, which he did. McNelly got back 400 cattle bearing the brands of ranches across South Texas, including many from the King Ranch.

McNelly had already been celebrated in Texas as a hero for his daring Civil War exploits in Louisiana and Mississippi. Now, at 31, he gained new celebrity as a hero for having stood up to Washington again — even though, this time, we were supposedly all on the same side.

FOR FURTHER READING: Taming the Nueces Strip: The Story of McNelly's Rangers, *by George Durham, as told to Clyde Wantland.*

HOW TEXAS SAVED THE BUFFALO

If it weren't for Texas, there would be no buffalo in Yellowstone National Park. Let me say that again. If it were not for Texas, there would be no buffalo in Yellowstone National Park.

I know that is a large claim, but it is not one that is without merit. I can back it up.

To be fair now, Texas had considerable liability for driving the poor buffalo to near extinction in the first place.

But once the forces of sanity took over and people realized that the range just wouldn't be as happy a home if the buffalo didn't roam, Texas took a lead role in saving these magnificent creatures.

In 1902, the U. S. Army estimated that there were just 23 buffalo left in Yellowstone. And they believed that number might be all the buffalo that remained in the wild, wild West. Imagine, just 23 buffalo left in the wild when 100 years before there had been many millions of them on the American plains.

Despite efforts to protect the 23 left in Yellowstone, the poachers poached away. After all, one impressive buffalo head could fetch $2,000 dollars to forever gaze back at patrons across a bar in Chicago. That's $20,000 in today's dollars. So the profit was high and the risk minuscule. This was the reality that seemed to doom the buffalo.

So how did Texas lead the way to saving them? To rebuild its buffalo herd, Yellowstone needed some good, pure buffalo bulls, and it needed them fast. The problem was that most of the buffalo then in captivity were cattalo, a mixture of buffalo and cattle. But in Texas, the famous cattleman Charles Goodnight, a man who cast a large shadow over Texas history, had his own herd of buffalo. Goodnight owned more than a million acres of land in the Texas Panhandle. The herd had been assembled by his wife, Mary Ann Goodnight, who personally saw to it that any orphan buffalo found wandering the ranch were saved and protected.

The Goodnights saved them from the Comanche Indians, they saved them from the Buffalo Bills of the world, and they saved them from wild predators of all kinds. So Goodnight, at his own expense, sent three fine, pure bulls up to Yellowstone to help rebuild the herd.

It worked. Today that herd numbers about 4,000, thanks to Goodnight. True, the U.S. Congress did create the Yellowstone preserve, and that was essential to the buffalo's survival. The U.S. Army did its part to help protect the Yellowstone herd from poachers in that enormous park, and that helped. But it was Goodnight providing the seminal gift, the breeding power, that truly saved them. And if you add to the count the buffalo herd Goodnight donated to Caprock Canyons State Park in Texas, you can say that Texas is largely responsible for bringing the buffalo back from the brink of absolute extinction. And that's no bull.

FOR FURTHER READING: Last Stand: George Bird Grinnell, the Battle to Save the Buffalo, and the Birth of the New West, *by Michael Punke.*

LARGER-THAN-LIFE TEXANS

JUDGE ROY BEAN: LAW WEST OF THE PECOS

Texas has produced and nurtured a great number of colorful characters, but none more colorful than the prismatic Judge Roy Bean. He squeezed many showy lives into one lifetime. In fact, he didn't become the Judge Roy Bean that Paul Newman immortalized on film until he was past middle age. This proves my favorite maxim: "The greatest mistake in life is thinking it's too late."

Kentucky-born (accounts of his birth date vary from 1825 to 1835), he was peripatetic in his younger years, moving from New Mexico to Mexico to California (San Diego and then San Gabriel) and then back to New Mexico during the mid-1800s, often following one or the other of his older brothers. Wherever he stopped, he was apt eventually to move on after brushes with the law, narrow escapes or other troubles. Finally, during the Civil War, he settled in a poor area of San Antonio, around South Flores Street, where he continued his notoriety. His disreputable schemes and exploits often made the papers, according to a recent *San Antonio Express News* feature, with one headline referring to him as "Scoundrel Bean." Eventually the neighborhood took its name for him: It was called Beanville. The Hispanics called him *Frijoles*. He had dropped his first name, Phantly, early on and went by his middle name of Roy.

In San Antonio Roy and his brother Sam had a business hauling freight (and weapons from Mexico for the Confederate Army). Roy married a teenager and commencing having children; he was arrested for aggravated assault against his wife, according to some reports, a year into his marriage.

To supplement the marginal freight business — one customer described his team and wagons as "the sorriest I have ever beheld" — he tried and failed at many things. He failed at selling firewood because he cut down trees that didn't belong to him. He failed as a butcher because butchering other people's maverick cows before you've bought them is frowned upon. He failed at selling milk because he watered it down. One apocryphal story has a customer complaining that he found a minnow in his milk and Bean defending himself by saying, "That's the last time I let that cow drink out of the creek before I milk her." He opened a saloon in Beanville, but when he heard there were rare opportunities out in West Texas where they were building the transcontinental railroad, he sold out to try his luck there, leaving his divorced wife and children behind. Most accounts agree that his more respectable neighbors encouraged his departure.

It was in the lawless railroad camps near the Pecos River that Bean's vast knowledge of people, his bilingual fluency in Spanish and English and his unique persuasion skills became very useful. Bean set up a makeshift tent saloon in one of the camps that had sprung up as the track advanced, Vinegarroon. The Texas Rangers needed a magistrate to control the violent and unsavory elements that had collected around the rough railroad camps; Bean needed a living. The Rangers, known themselves for making their own law, liked his style. In 1882 the Pecos County commissioners officially appointed justice of the peace in those parts. He took to the role as if he'd been sent there from central casting. Bean made it known that *he* was the "Law West of the Pecos." He was actually playing on an older saying that went like this: "West of the Pecos there is no law; west of El Paso, there is no God." So at least, now, there was "law" west of the Pecos. He set up shop in another tent city near the Rio Grande, Langtry, and hung out a sign saying so (along with a sign offering cold beer).

Bean was also famous for saying "Hang 'em first and try 'em later." Though it certainly worked as a deterrent, it seems likely that he never was responsi-

Photo by Carol M. Highsmith, Lyda Hill Texas Collection

The Jersey Lilly in modern times.

47

ble for any actual hangings. In his carefully researched history *Judge Roy Bean Country,* Jack Skiles writes that "there's no evidence to suggest that Judge Roy Bean ever hung anybody."

There was no jail in Langtry, so Judge Bean would often keep accused criminals chained to a mesquite tree outside until he could have a trial. Most cases were settled by fines, which often fattened Bean's pockets. On a few occasions, according to Texas historian C.L. Sonnichsen, he would sentence a young man to hang for some generally un-hangable offense. The night before the hanging, Sonnichsen's book *Roy Bean: Law West of the Pecos* tells us, Bean would leave the lock open, allowing him to escape. The young criminal would never be seen in those parts again.

Bean's famous saloon there in Langtry was on the railroad right-of-way. He was technically just squatting there, but the railroad eventually created a legal arrangement so he could stay. He named his bar the Jersey Lilly in honor of the English actress Lillie Langtry, who was considered one of the world's most beautiful women at the time and was known by the "Jersey Lily" sobriquet. The enamored Bean once wrote to her and asked her to visit Langtry, Texas, which he claimed was named for her (it was probably named for a railroad engineer). She wrote back, the story goes, and said she couldn't come just then but would like to buy the town a water fountain. He declined her offer, as he said people in Langtry didn't drink water. Lillie Langtry eventually did come to see Judge Roy Bean, but she had to visit his grave. She was 10 months too late.

The stories about Bean's bizarre interpretations of his office are legion.

Bean had cunningly situated his saloon next to the Langtry depot, where the trains would stop to take on water. Many of the passengers would get down to have a drink at the Jersey Lilly. When Judge Roy Bean served customers, he never had change. So, if a customer paid for a 25 cent beer with a dollar, he wouldn't get the 75 cents back. If he complained, the judge would fine him 75 cents for disturbing the peace.

As stories about the judge got around, more and more people on the trains wanted to stop and get harassed by the irascible Bean. It was a bit like the cachet of being abused by the Soup Nazi in *Seinfeld,* or the popularity of the Dick's Last Resort bar/restaurant chain, which became famous with its shtick of having the staff insult the customers.

The Jersey Lilly was also where Judge Bean held court. So, naturally, according to the legend, you couldn't be on a jury if you didn't drink. Right in the middle of happy hour, you might say, he would assemble a jury and swear them in. The case would be presented, verdicts arrived at and sentencing pronounced, all within an hour or two. Often the sentence for misdemeanors was to buy a round of drinks for the jury. Bean was very patriotic about Texas, too, according to Sonnichsen. He often preceded sentencing with words like:

"You have offended the great State of Texas by committing this crime on her sacred soil... "

Bean's only law book was the 1879 Revised Statutes of Texas. He liked that one. Even though the Texas Legislature sent him updated new books every two years, legend has it that he burned them. Though he was more likely to sit on it than to consult it, he said he liked the old book better and he liked those laws better, too.

As a justice of the peace, he could marry people. He had no legal right to divorce people, but he did that anyway, Sonnichsen's book says: He believed that if he made the mistake of marrying them he should be able to correct the mistake by setting them free. Bean also officially pronounced people deceased. He sometimes merged his rituals for marrying and burying. He would use his official pronouncement of death as the last thing he said at a wedding: "I pronounce you man and wife. May God have mercy on your souls."

One of his most famous cases had to do with a dead man who fell off a bridge. Bean, the story goes, found $40 and a pistol on the body. He fined the corpse $40 for carrying a concealed weapon.

Bean rose to international prominence with his involvement in a prizefight between Bob Fitzsimmons and Peter Maher that was touted as the 1896 world heavyweight championship. Prizefighting, back then, had been declared illegal in Texas. The sport was just beginning to be organized, and a Dallas promoter had put this particular fight together.

Fans in El Paso raised a substantial purse with the idea of holding the fight either in their city or across the river in Juarez, so the Texas governor, who was rabidly opposed to boxing, sent Texas Rangers and other law-enforcement muscle to the border town to make sure it didn't happen. Such fighting was illegal in Mexico, too, though only a misdemeanor. Nonetheless, because of all the uproar about the possible fight, the governor of Chihuahua sent troops to Juarez as well.

Finally, in stepped Judge Roy Bean, ever alert for such an opportunity. He sent a telegram to the promoter saying he could stage the fight near Langtry, on a sandbar in the Rio Grande, between the two jurisdictions. Even if the sandbar were closer to the Mexican side of the river, it was still miles from any Mexican authority that would be able to stop it. The site of the fight, of course, had to be kept a secret to prevent authorities from sending in reinforcements.

So the whole menagerie of unlikely associates — boxers, gamblers, high-rollers from the East, Texas Rangers and spectators of all stripes — boarded a train bound for parts unknown. Bean met them at his rail-side saloon, sold everybody beer at the exorbitant price of a dollar each and then escorted them across a pontoon bridge to the sandbar. The Texas Rangers watched from the Texas side, satisfied that they had no jurisdiction in the matter. The fight ensued, and before the spectators could get settled in for a good long match, it was over. Fitzsimmons knocked out Maher in the first round. The fight lasted 95 seconds. But the big winner was Judge Roy Bean. He sold a lot of beer, and his name went out over the wires worldwide as the clever man who made the fight possible.

Judge Roy Bean lived his life in ascendancy, becoming elevated in his later years from a small-time con man and carouser of local notoriety to a folk legend. Had he died 20 years earlier, in 1883 instead of 1903, you never would have heard of him. I wouldn't be talking about him. His fame is still bringing some 40,000 visitors a year to Langtry, more than a century after his death. Not bad numbers for a dead man. You can be sure that, as a lifelong showman, he's grinning in his grave.

FOR FURTHER READING: Roy Bean: Law West of the Pecos, *by C.L. Sonnichsen*; Judge Roy Bean Country, *by Jack Skiles.*

TOM LANDRY: THE MAN IN THE HAT

TXDOT

A mural in Mission honors Tom Landry.

Tom Landry and Charles Schulz died on the same day: Feb. 12, 2000. *Detroit Free Press* cartoonist Mike Thompson honored them both with a cartoon showing them entering the pearly gates together. Schulz was depicted as Charlie Brown; Landry had an arm around him and was saying, "Now, a few pointers on kicking a football . . ."

For Coach Landry, at least, I can't imagine a finer eulogy.

I mourned Landry's passing along with millions of other fans. A day that was almost as tough, though, was the day Landry was fired, in 1989. That day, too, hit me like a death in the family. Landry had been *our coach* since many of us were children. He had been our father on the field. He raised us within the game, teaching us to be gracious in victory and dignified in defeat. And with one stroke of Jerry Jones' pen, he was gone. Devastating.

Landry was known as the man in the hat. He was the stoic leader on the Dallas Cowboys sidelines, always impeccably dressed, sporting his fedora. Commissioner Paul Tagliabue said at one of his memorial tributes: "If there were a Mount Rushmore for the NFL, the profile of Tom Landry would have to be there, wearing his trademark hat for all of us to marvel at."

While coaching, Landry was so focused he rarely smiled. He was often called "unemotional." But I can think of words that would be more fitting: a

50

man of character, honor, integrity and faith. He was pure class, on and off the field. He was ethos personified.

In his 29 years as Dallas' head coach, Landry led the Cowboys to more playoff seasons, by far, than they have had since. And here is another statistic hard to fathom: The Cowboys still have not won as many games without Landry as they won with him. His playoff victories far exceed the post-Landry Cowboys' record too.

Under Landry, the Cowboys won 13 divisional titles and played in five Super Bowls, winning two. They enjoyed 20 consecutive winning seasons, a record no NFL coach has ever come close to matching, before or since.

As glorious as those years were, none equaled Landry's finest season in football. He played for the New York Giants professionally and was All-Pro one year, but that was not his finest season, either. He had played football on scholarship for the University of Texas, but neither were those his finest football years.

Something truly unexpected happened when Landry was in college. After only one semester, his career at UT was put on hold by World War II. After his brother was killed in action, he volunteered to join the Army Air Corps. Over the course of the war, he flew 30 missions over Germany, crash-landing once in Belgium. Though the wings were shaved off his B-17, he and all his men walked away without serious injury. He was only 20 at the time.

One could consider his WWII service, in a Churchillian sense, his finest season, but as we are talking football, we have to go back further.

To get to his best season ever, we have to go all the way back to his high school years in Mission, Texas, way down in the Rio Grande Valley.

It was Landry's senior year, 1941. He played both sides of the ball. He played quarterback and defensive back. Landry led the Mission Eagles to a perfect 12-0 season. They went all the way to the regional championship, which was as far as they could go that year (there was no state championship game in '41). They dominated Pharr San Juan Alamo in the district game, 33-0. They beat Aransas Pass for bi-district, 19-0. In the regional game, they demoralized Hondo, 33-0. Their fans followed them everywhere and were so devout they were called "The Missionaries."

The Mission Eagles won every game they played that year, holding every team scoreless except for one. In 12 games, they gave up only one score, and that was when Donna High School managed to squeeze out one touchdown against them. That touchdown was ironically awarded because of a pass-interference call against Tom Landry. But the touchdown was improperly given to Donna because the referee just gave Donna the touchdown, putting the points on the board instead of placing the ball on the one-yard line and awarding Donna a first down. In later years, Landry's high-school teammates would good-naturedly tease Landry about the irony of his being the one to make it to the pros when he was the weak link in their golden season.

In his autobiography, Landry wrote, "That autumn of glory, shared with my boyhood friends and teammates, remains perhaps my most meaningful season in 50 years of football. The game was never more fun, the victories never sweeter, the achievement never more satisfying."

Landry's near-flawless season, along with his impressive professional life thereafter, was honored in 1975 when the Mission School District named their football stadium the Tom Landry Stadium. After he died in 2000, Interstate 30 between Dallas and Fort Worth was named the Tom Landry Highway.

To me, one of the minor truths about Landry that speaks to his greatness is that his Cowboys never gave him a Gatorade bath, never dumped the ice bucket down his back. Too much respect, I suppose.

After his coaching days were over, he developed a sterling reputation as an inspirational speaker. He always advised young players to keep their lives ordered in this simple way: faith, family and football. He was also fond of saying, "As of today, you have 100 percent of your life left."

He took his own words to heart. After he was fired, while the rest of us were squandering our energy being furious about the disrespectful way our icon was sacked, Landry was already moving on with his life.

He didn't waste time being angry or bitter. With characteristic optimism, he saw the silver lining. He said, "As a boy growing up in Mission, Texas, I always dreamed of being a cowboy. For 29 wonderful years, I was one."

FOR FURTHER READING: Tom Landry: An Autobiography, *by Tom Landry with Gregg Lewis.*

'I'M EDDIE CHILES, AND I'M MAD'

I can think of three classic Texas ad slogans that would be shortlisted in the Texas Advertising Hall of Fame if we had such a thing: There's Blue Bell Ice Cream's "We eat all we can and we sell the rest." There's "Don't mess with Texas," the anti-littering campaign of the mid-'80s and '90s that was one of the most brilliant public-service campaigns ever created.

And then there is my favorite: "If you don't have an oil well, get one. You'll love doing business with Western." This latter slogan was for the Western Co. of North America, owned by Eddie Chiles, the iconic hard-charging Texas oilman.

Chiles actually became known for *two* slogans that became catchphrases in Texas. The other was "I'm Eddie Chiles, and I'm mad."

Chiles was the quintessential conservative Texan of his era. He was born in the small town of Itasca, Texas. His was a rags-to-riches story fit for a Texas Horatio Alger. Admittedly, he did leave Texas for college, to attend the University of Oklahoma (what I call a study-abroad program), but I guess we can forgive him that because he got a degree in petroleum engineering and promptly returned to Texas to start his company.

He founded the Western Co. of North America, a petroleum-industry services business, with three employees and two trucks in Fort Worth in 1939 and built it into a multimillion-dollar company. After that, he owned the Texas Rangers baseball team for about a decade before selling it to a group of investors that included future President George W. Bush. That was in '89. But before he sold it he did us the favor of signing Nolan Ryan to a $2 million contract.

Chiles was a cantankerous, colorful, hard-nosed *bidness*man. He was politically to the right of Attila the Hun, though his signature line was ironically inspired by the 1976 movie *Network* and its crazed anchorman prophet Howard Beale's "I'm mad as hell and I'm not going to take this anymore!"

Chiles never saw the movie, but he heard the line and identified with it, according to a 1980 *Time* magazine article. He associated Beale's line with his own frustration over big government, although big government was, of course, not what Beale was so aghast over in the movie. So Chiles took to the radio waves in 1977, producing a series of political commentaries, sponsored by the Western Co., with a similar approach. His line was, simply, "I'm Eddie Chiles, and I'm mad." And then he would go off on a rant complaining about his three favorite topics: big government, big government and big government.

He would say something like, "I'm sad for the Americans who are trying to raise a family and buy a home while the liberals in Congress are spending more and more and destroying the American Dream. You need to get mad, too." He would always end by noting that the government should defend our shores, deliver the mail and stay the hell out of his business.

Chiles became a folk hero of sorts. "I'm mad, too, Eddie" bumper stickers started sprouting up all over Texas — all over the Southwest, actually. You would see smaller versions on hard hats, right up front. "I'm mad, too, Eddie."

He once said, "Let me tell you why I am mad. Forty years ago, I started the Western Co., and under the free-enterprise system I was able to build that company into an international organization with some 4,000 employees. Today, I'm afraid the opportunity I had no longer exists. During the last 50 years the liberal philosophy practiced by Congress has literally turned the American dream into a nightmare. And this makes me mad. Fighting mad. I love America, and I'm determined to fight to get our freedoms back."

Chiles eventually had his political-commentary commercials running on 650 radio stations in 14 states where the Western Co. had operations. Because they contained plugs for the Western Co., he told *Time,* he deducted their cost as a business expense. This was at a time, in the late '70s and early '80s, when Rush Limbaugh had yet to find his niche as a radio ranter. Eddie paved the way for Rush Limbaugh and Sean Hannity, and possibly for the political career of Donald Trump. Some say he was instrumental in turning Texas red for Reagan in 1980.

Probably more people remember his "I'm mad" line than the slogan promoting his oil-services company. But I, for one, will always remember the ad that ran so often during NFL football games. A beautiful young woman would be standing next to a derrick, wearing a hardhat, and she would say, "If you don't have an oil well, get one; you'll love doing business with Western."

THE QUEEN OF THE KING RANCH

When Richard King, the founder of the King Ranch, died in 1885, his ranch holdings consisted of about half a million acres in the forbidding area of South Texas known to some as the Wild Horse Desert and to others as *el Desierto de los Muertos*, the Desert of the Dead. All his life, King maintained, he had faithfully followed the advice of his old friend Robert E. Lee: Buy land and never sell.

His wife, Henrietta, was 53. They had been married 31 years, and she knew that keeping the land was his highest priority. She did not let him down. She ruled this ranch kingdom for about 10 years longer, in total, than her husband did, more than doubling the size of the ranch in her time.

But it wasn't easy. She had to break her husband's golden rule soon after he died. Henrietta inherited not only half a million acres, but also half a million dollars in debt. She had to sell some of the land to bring the King Ranch back to life. Under Henrietta King's firm but fair hand, and with the expert help of her son-in-law, Robert Kleberg, the ranch was soon growing again; then flourishing. By the turn of the century, the King Ranch was trying new techniques in irrigation, range grasses and cattle breeding. By the 1920s, Henrietta's grandsons had created their signature breed, named for the creek and the Spanish land grant that lay at the heart of the King land: Santa Gertrudis cattle.

Henrietta Chamberlain met Richard King when she was just 18 years old, in Brownsville. She was the quiet daughter of a Presbyterian minister; he was a hard-drinking, rough-around-the-edges riverboat captain. When they married, in 1854, their first home, while the main ranch house was being built, was a stick-and-mud hut, "a mere jacal as Mexicans would call it," Henrietta wrote in her memoirs.

"But I doubt if it falls to the lot of any a bride to have had so happy a honeymoon. On horseback we roamed the broad prairies. When I grew tired my husband would spread a Mexican blanket for me and then I would take my siesta under the shade of the mesquite tree."

Henrietta King showed from the first that she was made of the right stuff to help build a ranch out of inhospitable land and a brutal climate. Historians agree that her husband, who was "largely unread," depended on her in much of the ranch's business. She took on the task of providing housing and education for the families of the *vaqueros* the ranch employed. And Henrietta was nobody's pushover. According to an obituary cited in a 2011 *Texas Monthly* article, "the outlaws and renegades who infested the neighborhood preferred to approach the house when Captain King was at home rather than try it when his wife was there alone."

She continued to reign faithfully over the ranch for 70 years, and her influence extended well beyond the King Ranch boundaries.

It has been said that the work of a philanthropist is like that of an old person who plants trees: They plant even though they know they will never live to stand in their shade. And so it is that the institutions Henrietta King started are far more important today than they were in her time.

Kingsville is built on land that Henrietta donated; working closely with Victoria architect Jules Carl Leffland, she financed the design and construction of the city's public high school. She supported the building of several churches; invested in a number of local industries; and donated the land for South Texas State Teachers College, which would become Texas A&M University Kingsville. In Corpus Christi, Spohn Hospital would not have existed without her donations.

It has been said that you can tell the importance of a person by the size and nature of their funeral. When Henrietta King died in 1925 at the age of 92, 200 vaqueros on horseback escorted her funeral carriage to the cemetery. Some of these ranch workers — known as *Los Kineños*, or the King's men — had ridden two days across the ranch, which now spanned 1.2 million acres, to get there in time.

At her grave, each of those vaqueros, one by one, circled her casket as it was lowered, and they tipped their hats in reverence for the great lady, *La Reina* — the queen of the King Ranch.

— *Co-written by Leah Scarpelli*

FOR FURTHER READING: The King Ranch, *by Tom Lea; Texas State Historical Association, tshaonline.org.*

SAMUEL WALKER:
THE REAL 'WALKER, TEXAS RANGER'

One of the most fascinating Texas Rangers of all time was Samuel Hamilton Walker — no relation, we should say right off the bat, to Chuck Norris' fictional character Cordell Walker. Many Ranger aficionados rate Sam Walker the second-most-important Texas Ranger of all time, behind Jack Coffee Hays, with whom Walker rangered. Now that's a dream team.

Samuel Walker arrived in Texas six years after Texas had won its independence. In five more years, in 1847, he would be dead. But in those five years he would defend San Antonio from Mexican forces, invade Mexico four times, escape from a Mexican prison and help design one of the most famous guns in history, the Colt Walker six-shooter (see "The Texas Rangers and the Colt Six-Shooter," page 41). When he died, he died in the quest to secure Texas' freedom from Mexico forever.

Born in Maryland in 1817, Walker had done carpentry work, spent a tour in the U.S. Army and worked as a scout in Florida before showing up in Galveston in 1842. He joined a Texas militia company and saw action in South Texas against Mexican troops under Capt. Jesse Billingsley and Alexander Somervell.

As a scout for Billingsley, he fought against Mexican troops in San Antonio. With the Somervell expedition later in 1842, he helped secure Laredo and continued on toward Guerrero, where word came that the Mexican army was on its way toward the company. Somervell ordered the troops to return to San Antonio. Among those who decided to heed the order were most of the Texas Rangers in the company, including Jack Coffee Hays, but about two-thirds of the men, including Walker, ignored the order and decided to continue on in a raid across the Rio Grande.

Their target was the Mexican town of Mier. When a much larger army of Mexican troops engaged them in defense of the city, the outnumbered Texans fought but eventually surrendered, and 180 Texans were taken as prisoners. They were marched to Salado and then toward Mexico City; en route, they effected an escape, but almost all the Texans were recaptured. As punishment for the escape, Santa Anna ordered them all shot, but cooler heads in the Mexican government prevailed and ordered decimation instead: One in 10 would die. The Texans were ordered to draw a bean from a pot. Among the white beans in the pot were 17 black ones. Those who got a black bean would be executed on the spot; those who drew white beans would live. Sam Walker got a white bean.

The prisoners who were spared were marched 800 miles across Mexico's brutal deserts. Walker mentioned in his journal of the Mier Expedition that he would not trade Texas for 100 Mexicos. He was however, impressed with the fine architecture he encountered in the churches of San Miguel de Allende, which remains true for the many expatriate Texans who live there today. Once in the capital, some of the prisoners, including Walker, were imprisoned at Tacubaya, a suburb of Mexico City, and some were marched another 100 miles and incarcerated in the infamous Perote Prison.

Walker's group was forced to do road work, including building a road from Mexico City to Santa Anna´s summer villa, which further enraged Walker. This amounted to a lot of salt in a deep wound, and he nurtured his loathing for Santa Anna — indeed, for all Mexicans — all his life, so much so that his friends called him "mad Walker."

There is a much-shared myth about Walker's time imprisoned in Mexico. The story goes that he was ordered to dig a hole for a flagpole and forced to raise the Mexican flag over the prison. According to one version of the legend, he put a dime at the bottom of the hole before erecting the flagpole and vowed to return one day to reclaim the dime. Several years later, the story goes, when he returned with American forces to occupy Mexico, he would take down the pole, retrieve his dime, reset the pole and raise the American flag in its place. It's a dashingly romantic story, and I wish it were true, but it is almost certainly apocryphal. First, Walker never mentioned it in his journals; second, the flagpole in the various versions of the myth is always in Perote Prison, in the state of Vera Cruz, and Walker was never incarcerated there. He was, however, part of Winfield Scott's invasion force that sacked the prison in 1847, and that may well be where the legend has its origins.

Walker eventually escaped from the Tacubaya prison — a story that would make a good novel in itself — and made it back to Texas. He joined up with Jack Hays and the Texas Rangers in 1844 and fought in many of the most famous Indian battles.

When Gen. Zachary Taylor sent out a call in 1845 for volunteers to scout for his federal troops, Walker immediately signed up. He ran messages through the Mexican lines to keep Fort Texas (soon to be Fort Brown) aware of Taylor´s plans for invading Mexico. Walker led the charge in the battle for Monterrey.

It was after Taylor's forces had secured Monterrey, in 1846, that Walker took a brief furlough and traveled back east. There he gave Samuel Colt some ideas for improving Colt's earlier model of his revolver called the Paterson pistol. Colt, in gratitude, named a special, very heavy model of his new six-shooter after Walker (see "The Texas Rangers and the Colt Six-Shooter," page 41).

Walker next joined up with Gen. Winfield Scott's campaign to attack Mexico City. Though he was officially made a U.S. soldier, everybody still thought of him as a Texas Ranger and called him Ranger Walker. Scott's army invaded Mexico at Vera Cruz and advanced from there toward Mexico City.

On the way, they sacked Perote Prison, released the prisoners and turned it into a fort for the American forces.

But Walker would not live to make it back to Texas. He was to die a few months later, fighting the army of his old nemesis, Santa Anna, at the town of Huamantla, where Santa Anna had positioned his forces to stop the U.S. troops' march to rescue the American garrison under siege at Puebla. Walker led his company, which was ahead of the main U.S. force, into battle there. His men fought fiercely until the main force arrived to defeat Santa Anna, but Walker didn't get to enjoy the victory. He lay dead; his prized Colt Walkers at his side. He was 32. In retaliation, his men went on a wild rampage, sacking, looting and pillaging the town.

Walker's body was returned to San Antonio; eventually it was interred in the Odd Fellows Cemetery next to the unidentified remains of the defenders of the Alamo.

It's said that Walker was not a man you would much notice in everyday life. He was of average size, and quiet. But in battle he was a lion. In his *Notes of the Mexican War 1846-1848*, J. Jacob Oswandel observed of Walker that "war was his element, the bivouac his delight, and the battlefield his playground."

FOR FURTHER READING: Samuel L. Walker's Account of the Mier Expedition, *by Marilyn McAdams Sibley.*

THE ORIGINAL 'MAVERICK'

This is a biography of a word. It is about a word that was born in Texas as a simple noun, grew up to achieve success here and eventually became famous the world over.

The word is "maverick," and it got its start in San Antonio, Texas, more than 150 years ago.

It's a word that is firmly ensconced in American culture: James Garner played Maverick in the beloved TV Western series of the '50s and '60s; Tom Cruise's fictional pilot in *Top Gun* was nicknamed "Maverick," and so was the real Sen. John McCain; in Texas we have the world champion Dallas Mavericks basketball team. The word means one who shuns custom, a lone wolf, a person who blazes his or her own trail and is willing to go against the crowd, an independent thinker.

Those are the more symbolic meanings of maverick, but most people know that the word's original meaning referred to unbranded cattle. Any cow that was unbranded was a maverick. What fewer people know is that the original herd of unbranded cattle that launched the expression was owned by a man named Samuel Maverick. Those unbranded cows were Maverick's cows.

That's how the term came about.

Some say that this was his clever means of claiming all unbranded cattle as his own.

But the fact of the matter is that Samuel Augustus Maverick was not all that interested in cattle, according to his grandson, the New Deal congressman and progressive San Antonio mayor Maury Maverick Sr. Samuel Augustus was a land baron, a real estate investor, as well as a lawyer who frequently held elected office. He was more interested in acquiring land than actively farming or ranching it. He at one time owned so much land in Texas that he ranked up there with Richard King and Charles Goodnight. There is even a county named for him — Maverick County. Eagle Pass is the county seat.

The cattle in question were a herd he had reluctantly acquired from a neighbor as payment for a debt. His grandson explained it on the floor of the U.S. House in 1938: "Many people have written to me and asked about the origin of the term 'maverick' as applied to unbranded cattle. This was not only one of the least of his accomplishments, but a mere accident. There is no romance to the story whatever — he merely had some 400 head of cattle that were left to roam in the wilds of Texas, under the care of a slave who never branded them. So people called them 'Maverick's cattle'; finally people called them 'Maverick's,' and then they were called 'mavericks.' Sam Maverick was never a cattleman, cared nothing for cattle, but it is true the great legend has grown up around his name. That is all there is to it."

I think it is a shame that Samuel Maverick became a household word for his unbranded cattle, because there are dozens of far more impressive ways that he demonstrated his maverick nature. He was a rare and unsung hero of the Texas revolution, not to mention having served his adopted state as a legislator and jurist. In so doing, he often lived up, quite impressively, to what his name would come to mean.

Samuel was a maverick from a young age. In his home state of South Carolina, everybody in the wealthy Maverick clan expected that Samuel, who had already launched a career as a lawyer with a degree from Yale, would take over one of his father's many businesses. But he didn't. He ran for the state legislature in 1830 and lost; his unpopular anti-nullification and anti-secession views — he did not think the state had the right to nullify federal actions — made him some enemies. In 1833 he left South Carolina, and by 1835 he had arrived in Texas to seek his fortune in a place where there was land aplenty to be acquired.

He got to San Antonio in 1835 as the winds of war were blowing. The Texas Revolution was brewing. No one was buying land then because no one was sure he could hold it — Texas was still part of Mexico, but for how long? Maverick bucked that trend. He jumped in quickly and bought huge tracts of land around San Antonio and further east along the Brazos. He seemed to believe in the old folk wisdom that you should buy land when no one wants it and sell it when everyone does.

He was plunged rather quickly into the revolutionary fray later that year when Gen. Perfecto de Cos' troops under the orders of Mexico's Santa Anna laid siege to San Antonio. According to Maverick's journal, he was placed under house arrest but freed when he promised to leave San Antonio and return to the United States. Once out of town, he joined the Texan resistance forces that were massing outside the city and helped guide Ben Milam in leading the attack to retake the city, which succeeded in routing the Mexican troops, at least for a couple of months. Thereafter, Maverick became a trusted and admired man in San Antonio and joined the Alamo militia.

In fact, he would have died at the Alamo had he not been selected by his fellow volunteers as their representative to sign the Texas Declaration of Independence in March 1836. He left for Washington-on-the-Brazos as Mexican troops were massing and arrived at the convention after the other delegates had signed the document. So he was a maverick when he added his signature a few days later to what the Mexican general Antonio López de Santa Anna, who had just wiped out all of Maverick's fellow troops back at the Alamo, considered a treasonous document.

After independence was won, Samuel Maverick served as mayor of San Antonio, again putting a target on his back as a leading citizen of a rebellious city. Santa Anna had not given up on getting Texas back and kept a list of those who were his enemies.

Sure enough, in 1842, six years after Texas had won its independence, Santa Anna struck again. He sent Gen. Adrian Woll across the Rio Grande, with orders to retake San Antonio and kill all those who took up arms against him. As soon as word got to San Antonio that Mexican forces had crossed the river, Maverick moved his family near La Grange for safety. He, however, had civic duties in San Antonio and so returned to the city. When Woll's troops attacked, Maverick organized a resistance force on the roof of his home. It numbered 53 men. Though they killed 14 and wounded 27 in the initial skirmish with the Mexicans, they were soon surrounded by 900 Mexican troops and forced to surrender.

Fortunately for Maverick and his compatriots, Woll did not carry out orders to execute them, probably because they were more valuable alive. He took many of these prominent Texans as prisoners instead and marched them back 1,000 brutal miles to Perote Prison in the state of Vera Cruz. One of them died along the way. Today, at San Antonio's Witte Museum, you can see the water gourd that sustained Sam Maverick during that grueling march across Texas and Mexico.

The prisoners were chained together in dark cells when they were not being subjected to forced labor. Maverick, as the representative of his men, asked for better conditions and was put into solitary confinement just for asking.

After a couple of months, Maverick was told that Santa Anna would offer him his freedom in exchange for signing a document saying that Texas had been illegally seized and should be returned to Mexico. Maverick refused. He wrote that he could not envision that any terms the Mexicans would make could be of advantage for Texas and that his loyalty to his country must win out over his desire to be freed. "I regard a lie as a crime, and one which I cannot commit even to secure my release; I must, therefore, continue to wear my chains, galling as they are."

While Maverick was in the dungeon, unbeknownst to him, San Antonians elected him as their congressional representative in the Republic of Texas.

Finally, in 1843, his release was negotiated by Gen. Waddy Thompson, a relation by marriage and the U.S. minister to Mexico. When Maverick left the prison, according to Paula Mitchell Marks' book *Turn Your Eyes Toward Texas,* he took with him the chains that had bound him all those long months as a lifelong reminder of the value of freedom.

— *With special thanks to Mary Fisher, great-great-granddaughter*
of Samuel Maverick

FOR FURTHER READING: Turn Your Eyes Toward Texas: Pioneers Sam and Mary Maverick, *by Paula Mitchell Marks.*

WILLIAM McDONALD:
THE MAN WHO GAVE US THE STARS

A few Christmases ago, I got to thinking about the great gifts, including both money and property, that have been given to the State of Texas over the years. I'm going to tell you about three such gifts that led to a priceless fourth.

In 1926, a bachelor banker died in Paris, Texas — a rich bachelor banker. His estate was worth about $1.2 million. Today, that would be about $17 million. In his will, the banker left most of his money to the University of Texas to buy a telescope and build an observatory.

The banker's name was William Johnson McDonald. No relation to the McDonald's hamburger chain.

Well, as you might expect, Mr. McDonald's relatives didn't like him leaving all that money for a telescope. Their stance was that anyone who would do such a thing must be, by definition, a bit crazy. So they sued.

Fortunately, Mr. McDonald's longtime interest in science was well-known — he had attended summer school at Harvard to study botany when he was in his 50s. He had even shared his dream of a giant telescope with his barber. Astronomy was a young science of great potential, should it receive the right funding, he said; indeed, he hoped that one day a telescope would be built that would allow astronomers to see the gold-paved streets of heaven. The university prevailed, ending up, after the litigation, with about $800,000 (which is still $11 million in today's dollars).

Once UT had the money, they had to go shopping for a mountain to put the observatory on. That must have been fun. Mountain-shopping has got to be something that you get to do only once or twice in a lifetime. Luckily for UT, they were located in a state that had West Texas in it, with some of the finest stargazing potential in North America. After driving several thousand miles around the region, inspecting various sites for altitude, dark skies, cloudless nights and poor prospects of rain, they found what they were looking for out by Fort Davis. It had no official name, but the locals called it Flat Top Mountain. It was part of a ranch perfectly named for that region: The U up and U down Ranch.

UT President Harry Benedict wrote a letter to the owner of that mountain, Mrs. Violet McIvor. He told her of McDonald's gift and of the university's great need for a mountain to put the observatory on. Benedict wrote that her mountain was ideally suited for such an observatory, that "optical tests already made showed that the Davis Mountains region was the best in Texas, perhaps the best in the United States, for astronomical purposes." He asked her if she might consider giving her mountain to science.

I think Mrs. McIvor surprised him when she did just that. She gave UT the entire top of the mountain, 200 acres, as well as the land to build a road to the summit. The resulting highway, Spur 78, has the highest elevation of any highway in Texas.

UT built the observatory and named it for William Johnson McDonald. The mountain was officially named Mt. Locke, after Violet McIvor's grandfather, G.S. Locke, from whom she had inherited it. She wrote to UT that she was delighted "to have her grandfather's name perpetuated in the Davis Mountains." She said, "He would have been pleased to leave his name among the mountains which he had known and loved so long."

I asked Mrs. Julie McIvor, who, along with her husband, Scott, still live on and operate the U up and U down Ranch, why her grandmother-in-law would have simply given away such a valuable piece of real estate, one that would be worth millions today.

"That generation was different," she said. "They believed in giving back. They were building a great state and a great country. She loved that she could do her part to empower a better future for Texas — and America."

As gifts inspire gifts, only five months after Mrs. McIvor donated her mountaintop to UT, the estate of longtime Fort Davis Judge Edwin H. Fowlkes, donated the adjoining mountain, known as Little Flat Top. The Fowlkes estate donated a total of 200 acres, and that mountain was formally named

Mt. Fowlkes in his honor. Mrs. Sheri Eppenauer, who is the granddaughter-in-law of Judge Fowlkes, told me he was a civic-minded man and always did what he thought was best for the people of Fort Davis and the region.

Three gifts to Texas: an observatory and two mountains. These collectively gave us a fourth gift — one of the world's leading centers of astronomical research. In fact, as McDonald predicted, these gifts gave us the heavens themselves.

— With thanks to Mrs. Julie McIvor and Mrs. Sheri Eppenauer
of Fort Davis, family descendants of the donors of Mt. Locke and
Mt. Fowlkes, respectively, for their kind assistance with this commentary

VAN CLIBURN: TEXAS VIRTUOSO

New York City has held more than 200 ticker-tape parades since the first one in 1886, which honored the Statue of Liberty. Charles Lindbergh got a ticker-tape parade for his solo transatlantic flight. Athlete Jesse Owens was celebrated for his four Olympic gold medals with a parade in 1936. World War II British Prime Minister Winston Churchill had a blizzard of ticker tape float down on him in 1946. The Apollo 11 moon landing team received a hero's welcome in ticker-tape in '69.

Of all the people and professions honored in this way over 130 years, only one has been a musician.

If you are thinking Elvis or Michael Jackson, you are way off base. The only musician ever to return to America as a kind of conquering hero was Harvey Lavan "Van" Cliburn Jr., a tall, lanky Texan who hailed from Kilgore. In 1958, he managed to pull back the Iron Curtain and thaw the Cold War for a few magical weeks. And he didn't do it with a Springfield rifle or a Sherman tank: He did it with a Steinway.

Nigel Cliff, the late pianist's posthumous biographer, says that his genius revealed itself early. His mom, Rildia Bee, an accomplished pianist herself, taught piano at home. She had just wrapped up her lesson with the last pupil of the day and said goodbye to him. She left the 3-year-old Van sitting on the piano bench while she went to fix supper. After 15 minutes she heard the piano and thought her student had come back, so she went back to the piano to hurry him home. The pupil was not there, but little Van was, playing the pupil's lesson by ear. His mother immediately made him one of her students.

At 10, Van told his mom and dad that his dream was to become a classical concert pianist. His father told him that, if he were going to be a pianist, he should be the best. He built a practice studio onto the garage of their ranch-style home and furnished it with a Steinway. There Van Cliburn practiced three to four hours a day. He would keep that Steinway until a year before he died, in 2013 in his adopted city of Fort Worth.

The young Van did have distractions along the way. As he had grown well beyond 6 feet tall before high school, the basketball coach came to recruit him. His mom told the coach that Van's hands were insured for a million dollars. No way he was going to risk them playing basketball.

Cliburn's mother took the teenage Cliburn to New York, where he attended some master classes at the famed Juilliard School, which offered him a scholarship. But he preferred his mother's tutelage, so back they went to Kilgore. Finally, at 17, he accepted a scholarship to Juilliard. Two years later, in 1954, he won the Leventritt Foundation award, which earned him debuts with five major orchestras. In 1958, at age 23, he agreed to compete at the inaugural Moscow International Tchaikovsky Piano Competition.

This competition was Russia's way of showing the world not only that they were the technological leaders, having put Sputnik, mankind's first satellite, in space six months before, but that they were also culturally superior to the decadent West.

The Russians were not expecting a tall young Texan to enthrall them with his mastery of Tchaikovsky and Rachmaninoff. Olga Kern, the celebrated Russian-American classical pianist, said, "Van Cliburn won because he played in a grand way. Soaring. It was beautiful; the piano was singing. It sounded so new and fresh. It was incredible." And when she visited his boyhood home in Kilgore years later, she said she understood where he got that style, because East Texas had enormous trees, vast fields and a natural sublimity that perhaps helped shape him.

Cliburn's reception in Moscow would have been the envy of any rock star. Women swooned. They cried over his powerful and fresh interpretation of Tchaikovsky. They brought flowers to the stage and laid them before the piano. It's been widely reported that the judges didn't know if they'd be allowed to award the top prize to an American, so they went to Soviet Premier Nikita Khrushchev himself and asked whether they could declare Cliburn the winner. Khrushchev is reported to have said in Russian what roughly translates to "Is he the best piano player? Then give it to him."

As the Russians opened their hearts to him, so did he to them. He had always been fascinated with the country, and he told a *New York Times* interviewer that the Russians had "reminded him of Texans."

And so Van Cliburn returned to New York a victorious cultural warrior. He was given a rapturous ticker-tape parade — the only one, ever, for a musician. He made the cover of *Time* magazine. The headline read: "The Texan Who Conquered Russia."

— *Co-written by Leah Scarpelli*

FOR FURTHER READING: Moscow Nights: The Van Cliburn Story: How One Man and His Piano Transformed the Cold War, *by Nigel Cliff.*

CHARLES GOODNIGHT

In the book and TV miniseries *Lonesome Dove*, Charles Goodnight was the inspiration for Capt. W. F. Call, played by Tommy Lee Jones (Goodnight also appears briefly in the book as himself). In truth, Charles Goodnight in real life was even more fascinating than the fictional Woodrow Call.

Goodnight, one of the most famous ranchers in Texas history, became a Texas Ranger at the age of 21. The Rangers recruited him because he was already locally famous in North Texas as a skilled Indian scout and tracker. The year was 1857, and the Texas Rangers and the U.S. Army were the front line of defense against Native American raids into Central Texas.

In his biography of Goodnight, revered Texas historian J. Evetts Haley relates numerous stories Goodnight told Haley about his days with the Texas Rangers. One was the story of how in 1860 the Rangers got an inexperienced commander from Virginia. This commander had never fought natives. He had never been out on the Great Plains. Yet he was puffed up with self-importance and wanted to charge out and take on some Comanches. So he ordered the Rangers westward, and after a couple of days he spotted his first Indians on a distant hill.

Excited, he called Goodnight over and asked him what kind of Indians they were. Goodnight looked where the man was pointing and replied, "Antelope." The rookie commander dismissed Goodnight's comment and ordered the Rangers to charge the group. "Which we did," Haley quotes Goodnight, "the old-timers roaring with laughter. And furthermore we put the bunch of antelopes to flight without the loss of a man."

Another story Haley tells about Goodnight turns on his fascination with the shields the Native Americans carried to stop arrows and bullets. One day he shot at an Indian retreating into the brush. His target escaped but dropped his shield. Goodnight took it back to the camp and pried open the buffalo-skin cover and wood frame and was shocked to discover an entire book inside. The book was *The History of the Roman Empire*.

That solved the mystery of why raiding Comanche so often took Bibles and other big books from whites when raiding. They wanted the paper to make their shields bullet-resistant. (They should have looked for *Moby Dick*. I always found that novel impenetrable. Don't know what it would do against bullets, but it makes a hell of a doorstop.)

Charles Goodnight was not only a Texas Ranger but also a business entrepreneur. Haley maintained that Goodnight and his partner Oliver Loving were the first to drive cattle from Texas to Colorado. (Loving, of course, was loosely depicted as Gus McCrae in *Lonesome Dove*.)

Everyone told Goodnight it couldn't be done. They told him he'd never be able to herd those cattle across the desert-like conditions of West Texas.

They told him he would be brutally killed by Apache or Comanches, staked out naked on an ant bed to wait for vultures to pick his bones. They told him that, even if he did make it, the cattle would be mere skeletons by then and he'd have nothing to sell.

Like all trailblazers, he simply ignored the naysayers. He proved them wrong and got rich doing so. It was 1866; he was only 30 years old at the time. As more Texas cattlemen followed his lead, and the trail became famous as the Goodnight-Loving Trail.

Goodnight eventually owned one of the biggest ranches in Texas, far exceeding a million acres. But, when he was in his 90s, biographer Haley reported, he had this to say about his tumultuous life:

"All in all, my years on the trail were the happiest I ever lived. There were many hardships and dangers, of course, that called on all a man had of endurance and bravery. But when all went well there was no other life so pleasant. Most of the time we were solitary adventurers in a great land as fresh and new as a spring morning, and we were free and full of the zest of darers."

FOR FURTHER READING: Charles Goodnight: Cowman and Plainsman, *by J. Evetts Haley.*

THE BASS BOAT HEROES

Every destructive hurricane is remembered in a unique way. Katrina, in 2005, is largely remembered for levees breaking in New Orleans and the paralyzing chaos that followed. The Galveston hurricane of 1900 is remembered for a horrific number: 6,000. Six thousand people perished. It was the deadliest natural disaster in United States history.

I think it's likely that 2017's Hurricane Harvey will be remembered for having dumped more water on a major metro area — Houston — than any other storm in U.S. history, but I believe it will also be remembered for the bass boat heroes.

Someone on social media suggested that we should build a monument to "two regular guys in a bass boat." That idea has been seconded by tens of thousands.

Even where I live in deep south Texas, I saw dozens of trucks pulling boats, headed north on U.S. Highway 77: bass boats, swamp boats, pontoons, skiffs and Zodiac inflatables like the military use. The call went out for help across the state, and Texans answered. They came from San Antonio and San Angelo and Austin, Waco, Dallas, Fort Worth, Tyler; even, I understand, from the Panhandle and El Paso.

From every nook and cranny of the state, they rolled toward the floods, spontaneous convoys racing to the coast. It was magnificent to see them: Texas flags bent by speed and proudly waving from their trucks and trailers, a genuine cavalry to the rescue. These men and women didn't ask for money or mileage or payback of any kind. They didn't ask for whom the bell tolled, they just concluded, it tolls for me — and away they went.

And they didn't just come from Texas. The Cajun Navy, as they are so beautifully named, poured across the state line from Louisiana in large numbers, as did others from Arkansas and Oklahoma, and no doubt other states too.

I talked to a man at a service station near my house who was filling up his GMC. He was pulling a 15-foot bass boat with a trolling motor. I asked him if he was going to Houston. He said, "My brother and me thought we might head up that way. I mean, I got a truck and a boat. Might be of help to somebody. I know they'd do it for us if things were turned around."

"These people are showing up with air boats, swamp boats and jet skis," A National Guard officer said on the Weather Channel. "They go out and rescue people and bring them to us. I don't know where these people are coming from, but it's the greatest thing I've ever seen."

An old friend of mine, Matt Carr, answered the call from Central Texas: "Driving into Houston in the storm was surreal," he recalls. "I-10, 290 and 610 had no cars on them. It was apocalyptic. Fields full of water, cows huddling on tiny islands above rising water. We felt all alone. We got there in a window of time before the world arrived again."

He said the police were swamped with emergency calls and told the rescuers they were free to go where they pleased and help in any way they could. So they did. Once the National Guard arrived, the process became more efficient. "It felt like a Texas version of Dunkirk," he said. "Less dangerous, but the same spirit."

Matt rescued a 90-year-old woman named Hazel. She lived alone in the Greenspoint neighborhood on the northern edge of Houston; she didn't have anyone in her life. She didn't want to leave her house, but she was cold. Matt persuaded her to go.

"I took her to a bus so they could take her to a shelter," he said. "She was scared. So I knelt down next to her in the aisle on the bus and we said a prayer together. And then I got back to work."

Matt's was one of thousands of similar stories from that night. My buddy Manny Fernandez, who is the Houston Bureau chief for the *New York Times*, witnessed several of his own. He was out riding along with many of these rescuers, impressed with their instinct for navigating what was now an urban bay. It was dark, except for helmet headlamps. Dangerous work.

Manny asked many of these rescuers why they had come so far to take these risks. Almost to a person, he said, they answered with three words: "This is Texas."

SCRIBBLERS, BARDS AND TROUBADOURS

McMURTRY, TWAIN AND ARCHER COUNTY

Larry McMurtry is, by many standards, Texas' best writer. He wrote *Horseman, Pass By* to wide acclaim in 1961, when he was just 25; two years later it became the movie *Hud*, starring Paul Newman. When he was 30, he published *The Last Picture Show*, which won him even greater critical praise; the movie that followed launched Cybill Shepherd's career. *Terms of Endearment* is another of his great novels; the film that followed pumped the book's sales when Jack Nicholson and Shirley MacLaine took the lead roles (although Nicholson's character is not in the book). Many would agree that McMurtry's best book is his Pulitzer-winning *Lonesome Dove,* and that became, to most Texans, anyway, the best television miniseries of all time.

McMurtry grew up on a ranch in Archer County, Texas, where there are about five people per square mile. A lot of people know that, but few know that another famous American writer owned land in Archer County. That was Mark Twain. He didn't live there — indeed, he never set foot in Texas — but he did own land there for a period, historical research tells us. It had belonged to his wife, Olivia, a soft touch who had loaned a woman to whom she was connected by family ties the money to buy some Texas land, with the property deed as security. The loan was never repaid, and Mrs. Twain ended up with the property. Twain inherited it upon her death and sold it a year later, in 1905. This 320-acre plot is still known by a few locals with long memories as "the Twain property."

Now let me stop here to tell you an interesting story about Twain and the land he owned in Archer County. One day he received a letter from the county clerk of Archer County saying that his land had been sold due to unpaid taxes. Twain had a man in Texas who was supposed to pay those taxes but had failed to do so. Twain reclaimed the land at a cost of twice the back taxes — $14.66. He was quite angry about the whole affair. He explained in a now-somewhat-famous letter to his friend William Dean Howells that the man in Texas who was supposed to have taken care of those taxes had taken the money and run, so to speak. If Twain ever caught up with him, he wrote to Howells, the scoundrel would suffer on a Biblical scale: "he shall beg for brimstone, he will beg in vain." Now there's a beautifully worded threat that even the Mafia could be proud of.

Many years ago I sent a copy of the Twain letter to McMurtry. I had stumbled across it in the Twain papers at Vassar University. I told him that he might be pleased to know that he wasn't the only famous author to have owned land in Archer County. He wrote back in his straightforward, modest style. He said that he hadn't known about that but was glad to know and that he would check into it to see if maybe they had owned some of the same land. I guess they didn't. I never heard any more about it. But the day I received that letter from the great man himself — that was a mighty fine day.

As a teenager, I used to lie awake at night reading McMurtry. I felt a special connection with him because we lived on the same road, U.S. 281. Six hundred miles apart, it is true, but on the same road. He lived a mile off U.S. 281 in North Texas, and I lived a mile off of U.S. 281 in South Texas. He could hear the trains where he was and I could hear them where I was. He and I were both lovers of books and of Texas. We both grew up in ranch country. He played the trombone. I played the trombone.

And, as the years passed, the similarities continued. He went to North Texas State, and so did I. He wrote a novel that won the Pulitzer Prize, and I . . . read it. He now divides his time between Archer City and Tucson, where I went to doctoral school and wrote my thesis — on Mark Twain.

Larry McMurtry is now in his 80s. Given the parallel nature of our lives, I'm praying he has many beautiful years ahead of him.

A DOZEN THINGS YOU MIGHT NOT KNOW ABOUT *LONESOME DOVE*

Lonesome Dove is the most persistently popular miniseries in television history. In Texas, it has the status that the Iliad must have had among the Greeks. Not too long ago I had a nice long chat with the man behind the miniseries, Bill Wittliff. He wrote the screenplay for *Lonesome Dove* and served as co-producer, too. After we talked, I came up with a list of 12 things you might not know about *Lonesome Dove*.

1. The original screenplay that would become *Lonesome Dove* was much shorter. That screenplay, in fact, was the seed of the novel. McMurtry wrote it in the early '70s with director Peter Bogdanovich, after their success with *The Last Picture Show*. It was called *Streets of Laredo* and was supposed to star John Wayne as Call, Jimmy Stewart as Gus and Henry Fonda as Jake Spoon. Wayne rejected the project, reportedly because he didn't like how the charac-

Robert Duvall was made an honorary Texas Ranger for his award-winning performance as Gus McCrae in Lonesome Dove.

ters of Stewart and Fonda would shape his role. In the end, Call was not the most likable of characters, and perhaps Wayne wasn't ready to play the "old cowboy" yet.

2. The *Streets of Laredo* script sat on the shelf for more than a decade, until one day McMurtry saw an old bus with "LONESOME DOVE BAPTIST CHURCH" inscribed on the side. He knew he had found his title. He went home and began reworking the story as a novel, inspired in part by the lives of Charles Goodnight and Oliver Loving. The novel won the Pulitzer Prize for Fiction in 1986.

3. The movie rights to the novel were bought by Motown, which made everyone stop and say "What's goin' on?" If it seemed an odd fit, not so. Motown producer Suzanne De Passe teamed up with Wittliff to produce a masterpiece.

4. Robert Duvall turned down the role of Woodrow Call so he could play Gus.

5. Duvall has said that, when they were making the film, he knew it would be a classic. He told his fellow actors, "Boys, we're making the 'Godfather' of Westerns." Later he said that he could retire from acting because Gus had been his Hamlet.

6. Bill Wittliff, the screenwriter, played a small role, as one of the sodbusters who was shot, hanged and burned.

7. Charles Bronson was supposed to play the brutal Blue Duck but had to back out due to contractual obligations.

8. *Lonesome Dove* did not win the Emmy for best miniseries in 1989. That honor went to *War and Remembrance,* which no one remembers. And not one actor from the miniseries got an Emmy. Robert Duvall, Tommy Lee Jones, Diane Lane and Anjelica Huston were all snubbed. At the Golden

Globes, however, *Lonesome Dove* won best miniseries and Duval best actor.

9. Gus' body, the mannequin Call brought back from Montana to bury in Texas, is available for viewing at Texas State University in San Marcos, which owns the *Lonesome Dove* collection. Curator Steve Davis told me that some people weep when they see Gus' body. You can also see Gus' hat and the blacksmith's poker that Call used to beat the "rude" Army scout to within an inch of his life.

10. Larry McMurtry wrote *Lonesome Dove* to explode our romantic notions about cowboy life and cattle drives. He wanted to show the brutal hardships and difficult times cowboys faced on the frontier. In this he may have failed. Woodrow F. Call and Augustus McCrae are now mythic characters and literary legends. They are admired and loved, in Texas at least, probably more than any cowboys in the history of Westerns.

11. *Lonesome Dove* has sold more DVDs than any Western in cinema history.

12. There is a longer version of *Lonesome Dove* — about 30 minutes longer — but we can't see it. It is locked away somewhere, and there are no plans ever to release it.

THE TOP 12 *LONESOME DOVE* QUOTES

Since I am, like many Texans, an amateur expert on *Lonesome Dove,* people often ask me what I figure are the most loved quotes from the miniseries. If I were wise, I would just say "any of a hundred quotes could be someone's No. 1," and leave it at that. But I have never let lack of wisdom stop me. I cannot resist the challenge of making a list. I know it is a delicate business. It's holy ground. However, the list I'm about to share is not just my opinion. I do have data on my side, feedback from a popular Facebook page devoted to *Lonesome Dove.* From that page I have been able to tabulate the most popular quotes or excerpts from the miniseries. I have 12 I will share, Letterman-style.

No. 12 comes at the end of the miniseries. Woodrow Call has just buried Gus and puts up the grave marker made from the old Hat Creek Cattle Company sign. Surveying the marker, he says: "I guess this'll teach me to be careful about what I promise in the future."

No. 11 is Gus McCrae 101. When the boys seem a little shocked by his, shall we say, manly appetites, he says: "What's good for me ain't necessarily good for the weak-minded."

No. 10 occurs right after Gus has cut the cards with Lorena and she accuses him of cheating. He says, "Well, I wouldn't say I did, I wouldn't say I didn't, but I will say this: A man who wouldn't cheat for a poke don't want one bad enough. Come on, darlin'."

No. 9: As Gus prepares to attack goes Blue Duck's camp to save Lorena, he says, "They don't know it, but the wrath of the Lord is about to descend on 'em, come sundown."

No. 8 is said the following morning. Gus finds July Johnson burying his stepson Joe, his deputy Roscoe and the girl Janey. July is distraught, blaming himself, saying he should have stayed with them. Gus tells him: "Yesterday's gone; we can't get it back."

No. 7 comes during one of Gus' many instances of exasperation with Woodrow Call. Gus says: "I God, Woodrow, you just don't never get the point, do you? It ain't dyin' I'm talkin' about, it's living."

The sixth-most-popular quote punctuates the scene when Jake Spoon is to be hanged along with the murdering horse thieves he has thrown in with. Jake pleads his case, but Gus has little sympathy. He says: "You know how it works, Jake. You ride with an outlaw, you die with an outlaw. I'm sorry you crossed the line."

No. 5 comes from the scene in the San Antonio bar that Gus, Call and Jake Spoon had frequented years earlier, during their glory days as famous Rangers. That scene has several great lines, so I decided to count them as one quote. The bartender, upon insulting Gus and Call, gets his nose broken when Gus slams his face into the oak bar. Gus tells him: "Now, besides the whiskey, I think we'll require a little respect. Now, if you care to turn around [nudging the barkeep's bloodied face in the direction of a photograph of the younger Gus, Call and Jake displayed behind the bar], you can see how we looked when we was younger and the people 'round here wanted to make us senators. Now the thing we didn't put up with then was dawdling service, and as you can see, we still don't put up with it." As they ride away, Woodrow tells Gus he's lucky he didn't get thrown in jail. Gus' reply: "Ain't much of a crime, whackin' a surly bartender."

No. 4 is a touching line, uttered by Gus as he lies dying: "It's been quite a party, ain't it?"

No. 3 is a tie. So close I couldn't separate them. The first comes at the first of the movie, back at Lonesome Dove when Bol implies that Gus may be too old for romance anymore and Gus sets him straight. He says, "The older the violin, the sweeter the music." Following soon after that scene comes Call's advice to Newt. Call hands him his first pistol and says, "Here. Better to have that and not need it than to need it and not have it."

In No. 2, Gus lays out a prescription for Lorie's future happiness. She is obsessed with finding her way to San Francisco, and he wants her to under-stand that achieving her dream might not be the only answer: "You see, life in San Francisco is still just life. Now if you want only one thing too much, it's likely to turn out a disappointment. Now, the only healthy way to live, as I see it, is to learn to like all the little everyday things . . . like a sip of good whiskey of an evening, or a soft bed, or a glass of buttermilk, or, say . . . a feisty gentleman like myself."

I began with Woodrow Call and will end with him at No. 1. Though Gus gets a great number of the best lines, Call gets the most powerful, most quoted line of all. Call has just beaten a thuggish Army scout to a pulp in defense of young Newt (who we know by then is, spoiler alert, the son Call has never acknowledged, perhaps even to himself). The townspeople, stunned by Call's explosion of brutal violence, stand paralyzed with shock. Indeed, Call himself seems stunned by what he has done and uncertain as to why he lost control. As the silence lengthens, Call finally says, stiffly, "I hate rude behavior in a man. I won't tolerate it."

There you go. That's the top 12 according to the data. Now, when you write to me to tell that the list is wrong or that I left out this or that, I ask only that you remember Captain Call's admonition: No rude behavior.

THE TIME IT NEVER RAINED

The great Texas meteorologist Isaac Cline is often credited with having said that "Texas is a land of perennial drought interrupted by the occasional devastating flood." Cline was assigned to San Angelo by the National Weather Service in the 1890s. He was delayed in reaching his post at Fort Concho by weeks because of swollen creeks and rivers. Drought followed.

It was a fellow San Angelo resident, Elmer Kelton, who years later wrote this often-quoted description of a West Texas drought:

It crept up out of Mexico, touching first along the brackish Pecos and spreading then in all directions, a cancerous blight burning a scar upon the land. Just another dry spell, men said at first. Ranchers watched waterholes recede to brown puddles of mud that their livestock would not touch. They watched the rank weeds shrivel as the west wind relentlessly sought them out and smothered them with its hot breath. They watched the grass slowly lose its green, then curl and fire up like dying cornstalks. Men grumbled, but you learned to live with the dry spells if you stayed in West Texas. There were more dry spells than wet ones. No one expected another drought like that of '33. And the really big dries like 1928 came once in a lifetime. Why worry? they said. It would rain this fall. It always had. But it didn't. And many a boy would become a man before the land was green again.

That is how Elmer Kelton's superb Texas novel *The Time It Never Rained* begins. The 1950s drought is a major character, asserting itself maliciously and unceasingly throughout the book. The central character is Charlie Flagg, a tough old rancher from a bygone era who refuses to take government aid to survive the drought:

Photo by Jeff Lynch

"There was a time when we looked up to Uncle Sam; he was somethin' to be proud of and respect, but now he's turned into some kind of muddle-brained Sugar Daddy givin' out goodies right and left in hopes that everybody's gonna love him."

To Flagg, "charity" is a shameful word. He rails against ranchers' getting too comfortable with government aid: *"It divides us into selfish little groups, snarlin' and snappin' at each other like hungry dogs, grabbin' for what we can get and to hell with everybody else. We beg and fight and prostitute ourselves. We take charity and give it a sweeter name."*

In Flagg's mind, when a rancher takes government help, as well intentioned as the government is and as deserving as the rancher might be, *"he's givin' up somethin' he can never get back. He's given up a little of his self-respect, a little of the pride he used to have in takin' care of himself by himself."*

If you asked me to list the top 10 Texas novels of all time, I could do it easily. Putting in them in order, though, would be a challenge beyond me. But I say for certain that somewhere in the top five would *The Time It Never Rained*. Spend a few evenings with Charlie Flagg and you will see the incomparable Texas spirit in its purest form. You will feel like you went out with your grandfather and checked to make sure all the fences were horse-high, pig-tight and bull-strong.

OSCAR WILDE TOURS TEXAS

One of the most-repeated quotations attributed to Oscar Wilde is this one, from "The Picture of Dorian Gray: ". . . there is only one thing in the world worse than being talked about, and that is *not* being talked about." He would be pleased to know that we're going to talk a good deal about him in the next few minutes.

Few people know that this great playwright, Oscar Fingal O'Flahertie Wills Wilde, the author of *A Picture of Dorian Grey* and *The Importance of Being Earnest*, lectured in Texas in 1882. He was just 27 years old, and on his first American tour.

When I first learned that Wilde had toured Texas, I was fascinated. I had been an admirer of his world-class, timeless wit since I was a teenager. So I immediately set about learning all I could about his tour here. That fascination resulted in a year of intense reading about Wilde's life, which inspired me to write an 80-page one-man play and to play Wilde in the production, in costume, four times. (It was actually a two-person one-man play because there was a 10-minute cameo for a prosecutor who cross-examined Wilde during the trial that famously ruined him. So I joked that it was the first two-person one-man show in the history of theater.) I wasn't an award-winning Oscar Wilde, but I do give myself some praise for being brave enough to be what Theodore Roosevelt called "the man in the arena." The play began with Wilde talking about his Texas tour, and that portion of the play became not only an academic paper called "Wilde Tours Texas" that I presented at a conference in Dallas but also this "Story From Texas" that I'm sharing now. Now back to our story.

Luckily, as his tour progressed, Wilde gave a lot of interviews to American papers, freely sharing his colorful and entertainingly phrased views on the people, places and levels of taste he encountered along the way. A couple of professors from the University of New Mexico collected those interviews in a book called *Oscar Wilde in America* in 2010, so we have ready access to his pronouncements.

At 27, Wilde was already enormously famous in Europe as a provocative personality, the leader of the aesthetic movement. He cut such a figure that Gilbert & Sullivan wrote an entire operetta lampooning him and aestheticism. When the operetta, *Patience,* was presented in America, Wilde was hired to promote it with a series of lectures on interior decorating. He was known for his affectations, including dressing opulently in purples and brocades, often with an eccentric sunflower in his lapel. So there was great curiosity in Texas about what would happen when this Irish dandy lectured in the macho world of Texas cowboys.

When he had passed through customs in New York City, he is famously (though possibly apocryphally) reported to have pronounced, "I have nothing to declare but my genius." Many Texans, being Tex-centric as we are, wondered what Wilde would think about their state. Well, for the most part, he liked Texas, as he told a reporter from the New Orleans *Picayune* upon his return there after his Texas foray.

As he took the train to Galveston, through East Texas and Houston, the *Picayune* reported, he was fascinated by all the alligators lying lazily on the muddy banks of the bayous.

His first Texas lecture was in Galveston, which was the largest city in Texas at the time. Oscar described it glowingly, telling the *Picayune* reporter: "Galveston, set like a jewel in a crystal sea, was beautiful. Its fine beach, its shady avenues of oleander, and its delightful sea breezes were something to be enjoyed."

He said, "The people of Galveston were wonderful to me. They made me an honorary Colonel in the Texas Rangers. So I wrote immediately to all my friends and told them that they should henceforth address me as Colonel Wilde."

From Galveston he traveled to San Antonio by train, in what he regarded as the monstrous Texas heat. (Incidentally, Wilde had noted of another excursion in the northeastern U.S. that traveling by train, whizzing by everything at 40 miles an hour, was no proper way to see new country. The proper way to see new country, he said, was on a horse.)

In San Antonio, Wilde stayed at the Menger Hotel, which of course still exists today. Even in 1882, the Menger was known for luxury, and so was Wilde, who famously said, "Let me be surrounded by luxury; I can do without the necessities!"

He toured the famous missions in San Antonio and proclaimed the San Jose Mission "the finest example of beautiful architecture I came across in all of the Americas."

He was quite moved by "those old Spanish churches with their picturesque remains of tower and dome, and their handsome carved stonework, standing in the verdure and sunshine of the Texas prairie."

As for the Alamo, though, he described the "noble" structure's condition as "monstrous." He thought it a shame that Texas had allowed this most "sacred of shrines to fall into such Philistine conditions." The Alamo had been, in those days, used as an Army depot.

He lectured in San Antonio on architecture and interior design, highly approving of the local use of the natural wood and stone that was so available in the Hill Country. When it came to interiors, though, he could be less enthusiastic. Often on his U.S. lecture stops he complained about the overuse of horrid wallpaper, noting that a child raised in the ambiance of such wallpaper could later use it as a "defense for a life of crime." (If this seems like an undue fixation on wallpaper, remember that Wilde's last words, famously, are reported to have been: "My wallpaper and I are fighting a duel to the death. One or the other of us has to go.")

When Wilde was asked in Louisiana how his lecture in San Antonio had gone, he replied that the women had loved it but the men not so much. Indeed, the men were quite a distraction, he told the *Picayune* reporter, "walking in and out with their squeaky boots and clangy spurs. The men were going out for beer, you see.

"Evidently," he said, "men in Texas cannot survive more than an hour between beers."

If he were to return today, 135 years later, he would likely find us about the same.

FOR FURTHER READING: Oscar Wilde in America: The Interviews *by Oscar Wilde and Matthew Hofer;* Declaring His Genius: Oscar Wilde in North America, *Roy Morris Jr.*

JULES VERNE, TEXAS AND THE MOON

The first word uttered on the moon that was intended to be heard on Earth was "Houston." That was the first word of the phrase uttered by Neil Armstrong after his and Buzz Aldrin's successful landing of the lunar module on June 20, 1969:

"Houston, Tranquility Base here. The Eagle has landed."

Before that announcement came a few words during the descent — "Contact light. OK, engine stop" — but those were part of the back-and-forth between the astronauts as they navigated the descent and landing. The first words meant for Earth were those that officially announced the safe landing of the Eagle on the moon, and those words began with "Houston."

The fact that Houston was so central to the success of the achievement had been foreshadowed, in a way, some 100 years before, by Jules Verne, in his novel *From Earth to the Moon.* This is, of course, the same Jules Verne who wrote *Twenty Thousand Leagues Under the Sea, Journey to the Center of the Earth* and *Around the World in 80 Days* — the father of modern science fiction.

Verne's 1865 book *From Earth to the Moon* concerns a moon shot. And it was actually a moon *shot,* because in the book the people behind the space effort were weapons enthusiasts — the Baltimore Gun Club — who wanted to build an enormous space cannon and fire a huge bullet at the moon.

Now, drawings of the bullet that illustrated the book make it look remarkably similar to the Apollo capsule. It had room for three people, just like the real lunar expedition that would come 100 years later. It was made of aluminum, which would be used in the Apollo capsule, too. Even the physics of

Verne's moon voyage were impressively correct for his time, all except for the intolerable g-forces that would have been experienced by the people in the bullet capsule. Verne, by the way, named his launch cannon the Columbiad. The command module for the moon landing was the Columbia.

So how does Texas factor into the book? Well, Verne calculated that the best place from which to launch such a shot at the moon would be found in either Texas or Florida. It would have to be near or below the 28th parallel. He discussed Brownsville as a possible launch site. (It's interesting that Space X is now building a facility there.) Corpus Christi was mentioned, and so was Galveston Bay near Houston. Verne named one site in Florida as an option, "Tampa Town." The real-life Tampa is just across the state from the Kennedy Space Center at Cape Canaveral, eventual site of the real moon launch a little more than 100 years later.

Some of Verne's other foreshadowing came in the area of politics. A Frenchman by birth and by residence, Verne made only one trip to the United States in his life, in 1867, to visit New York City and Niagara Falls. Nonetheless, he harbored a lifelong fascination with America, where he set not only this novel but more than 30 others. In *From the Earth to the Moon* he wrote a wonderful chapter about Florida and Texas each flexing their political muscle and persuasion skills to win the space launch. The same kind of thing, indeed, happened 100 years later. The debate was essentially settled by President Lyndon Johnson, Texas' native son. His political maneuvering led to the launch site being awarded to Florida and the command center to Texas.

It's fascinating to take a look at the arguments Verne had each state advance in his novel, which brings proponents of the two states together for a meeting at a hunting lodge. The Texans claimed a greater population — 330,000 to Florida's 50,000. Texas had the finest cotton, the best iron ore, the purest-grade oil and the most coveted green oak for ships. Tampa said they had the best bay from which to bring in supplies. Huh, Texans responded. "You mean a bay clogged with sand?" After all, the Texas side countered, "Galveston Bay can hold all the navies of the world!"

And then Florida dropped the big one: "The space launch should go to the state that is truly American." The Texans got red-faced: "Scandalous — wretched little strip of country like Florida to dare to compare itself to Texas. Texas didn't just lie down and sell herself to the Union for $5 million. She won her own independence at San Jacinto when Sam Houston defeated Santa Anna and drove the Mexican armies from the state" — after which Texas "voluntarily annexed itself to the United States of America."

Besides, the Texans argued, when it came time for the actual moon shot, that little strip of land called Florida "could never sustain the shock of the discharge; it would bust up at the very first shot."

"Very well, let it bust up," replied Florida.

The Florida side went on to point out that all the Texas sites were well below the 29th parallel and Tampa Bay was right smack on the 28th, perfectly positioned for the moon shot.

And so Florida won, at least in the book; a century later, it got the real launch site too.

In real life, though, I figure Texas got the best deal, because it got the command center (and the big budgets). And it got the first word. The first formal word uttered on the moon was not "Tampa," or "Florida." It was "Houston."

I can't help thinking that Sam Houston, the old backwoodsman and wily general, would have been proud to know that his name was at the forefront of still another revolution.

A YEAR'S WORTH OF TEXAS READING

I'm not an expert on many things, but when it comes to judging the quality of Texas literature, or Texana, as it is called, I am as confident as a bronc rider still upright at seven seconds. (That last second of the eight is reserved for humility: Chance needs scant time to have one spittin' up dirt.)

So I decided I would take my chances and prepare a list of good Texas books you might want to explore over a year of reading, one book for each month. Here we go:

January: *The Tacos of Texas,* by Mando Rayo and Jarod Neece.

This guide to all things taco in Texas by the Austin-based blogging team behind TacoJournalism.com became a best-seller in Texas (and beyond) after its publication in 2016. I assign it to January because by about Jan. 3 your New Year's resolutions will be somewhat less resolute. When that time comes, you will want tacos. And the tacos will give you strength for a fine year of reading ahead.

February: *The Son,* by Philipp Meyer.

To my mind, this ambitious tome is the best Texas novel since *Lonesome Dove.* It was first runner-up for the Pulitzer Prize in 2014. The miniseries aired on AMC in 2017 with Pierce Brosnan. But read the book and you will have the advantage of saying, somewhat snobbishly, "I read the book, and the book is way better."

March: *Miles and Miles of Texas: 100 Years of the Texas Highway Department*, by Carol Dawson and Roger Allen Polson.

Just in time for your spring break trip is this magnificent book on the history of Texas roads and how they got built. The original mission of the Texas Highway Department was to "get the farmer out of the mud." Obviously they went far beyond that goal in building a state of superhighways. Let's not talk about I-35.

April: *Lonesome Dove,* by Larry McMurtry.

Cattle drives in Texas typically began in the spring, so April seems like a good time to read or re-read *Lonesome Dove,* the *Iliad* of Texas. If you haven't read this Pulitzer-winning literary treasure, it's time. Gus and Call are waiting for you.

May: *Texas Ranger: The Epic Life of Frank Hamer, the Man Who Killed Bonnie and Clyde,* by John Boessenecker.

The notorious outlaw couple met their death in a police ambush on May 23, 1934, thanks to the subject of this book. Hollywood made Hamer out to be the bad guy, but, as is often the case, they were seduced by myth and got it wrong. I like what the *Dallas Morning News* says about this book: "Frank Hamer's is perhaps the last great story of the American West to be told . . . Well, Hollywood? Now you have the book, so go make the movie."

June: *Isaac's Storm: A Man, a Time, and the Deadliest Hurricane in History,* by Erik Larson.

For the start of hurricane season, read this best-selling history of the killer hurricane that devastated Galveston in 1906, centering on Isaac Cline, chief U.S. meteorologist in Galveston at the time of this deadliest of storms. "Gripping," said *The Washington Post,* ". . . the *Jaws* of hurricane yarns."

July: *Empire of the Summer Moon: Quanah Parker and the Rise and Fall of the Comanches, the Most Powerful Indian Tribe in American History,* by S.C. Gwynne.

This book tells the story of the last years of the Comanche Nation and how Quanah Parker and his warriors were never militarily defeated. *The New York Times* said it "will leave blood and dust on your jeans."

August: *The Time It Never Rained,* by Elmer Kelton.

Kelton's classic 1973 novel tells the story of a West Texas rancher, Charlie Flagg, who lived through the devastating seven-year drought in the 1950s that is considered the worst dry spell in modern Texas history.

September: *Friday Night Lights: A Town, a Team and a Dream,* by H.G. Bissinger.

The beginning of football season is the perfect time to read the nonfiction book about Odessa's Permian Panthers that launched the popular TV series. (If you've read it already, opt instead for Larry McMurtry's *The Last Picture Show,* which is also anchored in Texas football culture.)

October: *All the Pretty Horses,* by Cormac McCarthy.

Winner of both the National Book Award and the National Book Critics Circle Award. Once you're in, go ahead and read the whole "Border Trilogy."

November: *Lone Star: A History of Texas and the Texans,* by T.R. Fehrenbach.

As the days shorten and the nights lengthen, sit by the fire and read military historian Fehrenbach's unsurpassed chronicle of Texas from prehistory into the 20th century.

December: *The Big Rich: The Rise and Fall of the Greatest Texas Oil Fortunes*, by Bryan Burroughs.

Christmas will be upon us again. As you begin worrying about presents and money, it's an ideal time to read the rags-to-riches Horatio Alger stories of Texas oilmen like H.L. Hunt and Roy Cullen. These were men who became, for their time, among the absolute richest in the world. They knew how to spend money and to play on a scale few have ever known. It will inspire your Christmas shopping and make you want to play poker for oil leases, buy sprawling ranches and purchase your own Texas island.

There's not a lot of romance in these books. There is a lot of tough love, though. And that's good. If you don't get tough love early in life, it's hard to find lasting love later.

Happy reading.

TOP TUNES ABOUT TEXAS TOWNS

There are thousands of songs about Texas. George Strait's "All My Ex's Live in Texas" and "The Yellow Rose of Texas" are among the first that come to mind. Even all the way over in England, Duran Duran, the British new-wave synth-pop group, dropped a top-20 song called "Rio," about a girl who'd "dance across the Rio Grande," back in '82. "The Road Goes on Forever," sang Robert Earl Keen, as does the list.

Pat Green sang in "Songs About Texas" that "there's a song in every town," implying that every town in Texas has its own song. That could be true, but only a rare few made it to the Billboard top 40.

So I thought it would be interesting to look at Pat Green's idea with one proviso: What are the songs about Texas towns that became bona-fide hits? Not just songs about Texas, but songs about specific towns in Texas. I looked at songs after 1960 (when the charts were more reliable) that became hits on either the pop or country charts.

First is "El Paso" by Marty Robbins, his most famous song. It was released in '59 and hit No. 1 in January of 1960. And some trivia? The cantina beauty "Feleena" (Robbins seems to have been a little challenged in Spanish spelling) was named after a fifth-grade schoolmate, Fidelina Martinez.

I must also mention Robbins' "Streets of Laredo," which was an unofficial hit that same year — unofficial because it was never released as a single, though it received a lot of air time.

Next is "Galveston," sung by Glenn Campbell, which made it to No. 4 on the Billboard Hot 100 in 1969. Jimmy Webb wrote it while sitting on Galveston Beach.

"Is Anybody Going to San Antone?" made it to No. 1 on the country charts in 1970, as sung by Charley Pride. Written by Glenn Martin and Dave Kirby, the song was also made popular by Texan Doug Sahm, who recorded it twice: once in 1973 and again in '91 with the Texas Tornadoes.

The Doobie Brothers' "China Grove" was No. 15 in 1973. Tom Johnston, who wrote it, has told several interviewers he originally thought he'd made the name up but later found out there actually was a Texas town with that name. He thinks the name must have lodged in his mind subconsciously when the band was on tour in 1972 and drove by a road sign for China Grove, a town of less than 1,000, as the lyrics say, "down around San Antone."

The same year, 1973, saw ZZ Top's "La Grange." The song made it only to 41 on the Billboard Hot 100, but in Texas it no doubt ranked much higher. From the album "Tres Hombres," this song put the best little whorehouse in Texas, the Chicken Ranch, on the map — made it "nationwide," in ZZ Top lingo. It also made No. 74 on *Rolling Stone*'s list of all-time great guitar songs because of Billy Gibbons' virtuoso performance on a 1955 Fender Stratocaster.

"Luckenbach, Texas" was released in 1977 by Waylon Jennings and made it to No. 25 on the pop charts and No. 1 on the country charts, where it stayed for more than a month. I guess the idea of simpler country living was appealing. It made Luckenbach so popular the state had to stop making "Luckenbach" road signs because the theft rate was too high.

George Strait's version of "Amarillo by Morning" hit No. 4 on the country charts in 1983. Written by the songwriting team of Terry Stafford and Paul Fraser a decade earlier, the original version sung by Stafford had climbed to No. 31 on the country-singles chart and remained popular in Texas.

Some of my much-loved favorites, like Joe Ely's "Dallas" and "Gary P. Nunn's "London Homesick Blues," didn't make the cut here because they didn't make it big in Billboard. But I know they would've if there'd been Billboard record charts just for Texas all those years.

I have to end with a tip of the hat to "I'm a Ding Dong Daddy From Dumas." Though it was released before there were charts, it was a quite a phenomenon in the 1930s and '40s. It was written by pianist and prolific songwriter Phil Baxter, who led a successful Southern territory band called the Texas Tommies in the '20s. Carl Moore, a drummer and singer who performed with Baxter's band, is often credited as co-writer. The song caught on as a novelty hit and in the years since has been performed by everyone from Louis Armstrong, Sidney Bechet, Stuff Smith, Eddie Condon, Benny Goodman and Gene Krupa through Bob Wills, the Light Crust Doughboys, Asleep at the Wheel and Robert Earl Keen to the Royal Air Force Dance Orchestra Squadronaires and a group called the Nuclear Whales Saxophone Orchestra.

Bandleader Baxter was indeed born in Texas, in the bucolically named Rural Shade community near Corsicana, which is quite a ways from the Panhandle town of Dumas. Co-writer Moore was born in Arkansas, which also happens to have a town named Dumas. Both Dumases claim the song as their own, but the Texas Dumas' claim is arguably better-known. The town radio station is even named KDDD — for Ding Dong Daddy.

Go this web address and you can hear this commentary with the music: http://www.texasstandard.org/stories/categories/wfstrong/top-of-the-charts-all-the-hit-songs-about-texas-towns/

HOMESICK FOR TEXAS

To my mind, the signature song about longing for Texas is this one:
I wanna go home with the Armadillo;
Good country music from Amarillo and Abilene;
The friendliest people and the prettiest women you've ever seen.
That's "London Homesick Blues," sung by Jerry Jeff Walker and written by Gary P. Nunn.

But there are dozens of songs that make Texpatriates (Texans forced to live outside of Texas a while) a little misty-eyed. Here's George Strait:
Amarillo by morning, up from San Antone.
Everything that I've got is just what I've got on.
When that sun is high in that Texas sky
I'll be buckin' at the county fair.
Amarillo by morning, Amarillo I'll be there.
And what Texan isn't moved by these immortal words?
Let's go to Luckenbach, Texas,
With Waylon and Willie and the boys …
The theme of Texas homesickness is a common theme in our music, our folklore and our literature.

Did you ever hear the story about the Montana cowboy who died and went to Heaven? St. Peter was giving him a tour when the Montanan looked up to see a bunch of cowboys in jail, struggling to get out. The Montanan said to St. Peter: "I'm a little surprised to see a jail in heaven!"

St. Peter said, "Oh, that's not a jail. That's the Texas Detention Center."

Montanan said, "Oh I understand. I did some drovin' with those ol' boys. When they get to a new town they can do some damage."

"That's not the problem," said St. Peter. "The problem is they get so home-sick they keep tryin' to sneak out the Pearly Gates to go back to Texas. So we have to keep 'em locked up a while till they learn to like it here."

We find the theme in Larry McMurtry's work, too. In his little early mas-terpiece of a novel *All My Friends Are Going to Be Strangers*, the central char-acter, Danny Deck, is leaving Texas for the first time in his life. He is driving just west of El Paso and about to cross the border when he says, "It was strange, leaving Texas . . . It was all behind me, north to south, not lying there exactly, but more like looming there over the car . . . some genie, some god, towering over the road. I really felt it . . . I had left without asking permission, or earning my freedom. Texas let me go, ominously quiet. It hadn't gone away. It was there behind me."

When he returns to Texas after several months, Danny realizes what many a traveler has realized: That there is no place like home. He says, "It was the sky that was Texas, the sky that welcomed me back . . . The sky was what I had been missing, and seeing it again in its morning brightness made me realize suddenly why I hadn't been myself for many months. It had such depth and such spaciousness and such incredible compass, it took so much in and circled one with such a tremendous generous space that it was impossible not to feel more intensely with it above you."

I can't help but be reminded of what my brother Redneck Dave once told me: "I reckon everybody everywhere misses their home," he said, "but if there was a way to measure the mightiness of missin', I'd betcha big that Texans would come out pretty much on top."

I can't argue with that.

Photo by Jeff Lynch

ICONIC TEXAS

RATTLESNAKES

If you could put all of Texas culture into one football stadium, which would be a good place to put it, you would need to reserve a large section for rattlesnakes. After all, rattlesnakes have always loomed large in Texas legend and lore. A friend of mine from Austria tells me that, when Europeans think about Texas, they think of cowboys and cattle and oil and rattlesnakes.

This is not surprising at all. Seems like every Western ever made has a scene where a cowboy is surprised by a rattler and dispatches

Photo by George McLemore

it with one perfect shot from his six-shooter. Having grown up myself in the brush country of Texas, I never found a pistol to be all that certain. I preferred a shotgun, a 12-gauge if handy and a double-barreled if possible.

An old rancher told me that if I ever heard a rattler raisin' a warning nearby, I didn't even need to look or aim. Just move the barrel in his direction, the rancher said, and he'll aim for you. He'll line up his head with the end of the barrel, and you'll get him most every time. I didn't like his use of the word *most* in that prescription.

My mama had filled my head with all kinds of horror stories about rattlers. They could put their tail in their mouth and form a wheel to chase you with. If you shot one, he never died until the sun went down, and his mate was sure to be looking for you forever. "They are always hiding up under the truck," she said, "waiting for you to get out, so don't dawdle. Get in the house."

If you cut a rattler's head off, you should never carry the head in your pocket — because you could reach in that pocket absent-mindedly, days later, and still get bit. One boy who did that got bit and died.

And the rattles themselves were dangerous, because rattle dust could blind a person. My mom told me years later that she knew most of it was exaggerated — but, she said, you couldn't raise boys on reason; best to keep 'em scared.

The great folklorist J. Frank Dobie said that there were two measures to Texans' character: Did they close every gate they went through and did they kill every rattler they came across? Dobie regarded the snake topic as so important that he wrote an entire book about it. And, being a professor he gave the book one of those deep philosophical titles. He called it *Rattlesnakes*.

He spends some time on stories about the biggest rattlesnakes ever found in Texas. Several accounts going back to frontier Texas claim the existence of rattlers 10 and 12 feet long, weighing 25 to 30 pounds. Some speculate that such giants existed back then because human encroachment had not been a factor long enough to cut short their growth.

Such monster rattlers are not found these days, except for those ubiquitous pictures on the internet using forced-perspective techniques. At the Snyder and Freer rattlesnake roundups each year, six-footers are not uncommon, and once in a great while an eight-footer is brought in, but never 10- or 12-footers. Dobie says the best way to make records in rattlesnakes is to do it far away from measuring tapes and yardsticks — and with as few witnesses — as possible. Such things have a way, he notes, of "making one cautious with the facts."

IN THE LAND OF PICKUPS, TEXAS IS KING

To paraphrase Robert Duvall's Kilgore in *Apocalypse Now*, "I love the sound of a diesel engine in the morning." Could be a pickup or a tractor or an 18-wheeler — but I love the sound because it sounds like adventure. It is the sound that says we're off on a road trip, or going fishing or hunting, or simply taking livestock to auction, to make more money for more adventure.

They're not all diesel, of course, but Texas buys more pickup trucks than any other state. In fact, there is not even a respectable second place. You'd have to add California and Florida and Oklahoma together to get a respectable second place in truck sales. And, if Dallas and Houston were a state, *they* would be No. 2 in truck sales, behind the rest of Texas. That's a lot of trucks, y'all.

One-fourth of all new vehicles sold in Texas are pickup trucks. Texas is so dominant in truck sales, in fact, that auto companies sometimes divide their national marketing into four districts: North, East, West and Texas. Hence the slogans "Built Texas tough" and "Built by Texans for Texans" you hear in so many ads.

Pickups are the luxury cars of Texas. In Texas the No. 1 status symbol is not a Mercedes or a BMW, it is a big, powerful, fully-decked-out pickup like a Ford F-250 or Chevy or Dodge Ram 2500, with a Power Stroke, Duramax or Cummins Diesel.

The flagship truck for Texas appeal is Ford's King Ranch Edition pickup. Everybody knows that the King Ranch is the biggest ranch in Texas. It was a stroke of marketing genius when Ford wrapped its truck in the manly ethos of the King Ranch brand for the 2001 model year. Every leather seat within the truck is emblazoned with the King Ranch "Running W" cattle brand, an icon of Texas macho.

The King Ranch, as it turns out, uses only Ford trucks. It has about 350 of them throughout its various divisions, William J. Gardiner, who is senior vice president and CFO of the ranch, told me.

One out of every five trucks Ford sells is purchased in Texas, and the King Ranch edition pickup is the best-selling of all Ford's specialty brands, according to the financial website Motley Fool. Some 40 percent of the King Ranch models are sold in Texas, leaving a respectable 60 percent for those across North America who want to feel a little bit Texan every time they drive. Ford is not alone in the specialty market. Chevy and GMC have Texas editions; so does Ram, with its Lone Star Edition, available new only at Texas dealerships; and so does Toyota, whose full-size pickups are all built in San Antonio.

As long as truck companies are into specialty models, I have a couple of suggestions: The South Padre Edition, featuring large beach tires, a tailgate grill and a surf pole rack on the front as standard equipment. Or a Big Bend Edition, whose standard features would be off-road tires, a 12-inch factory lift kit, and a front bumper winch. I don't expect royalties. Just a free truck.

Country music, of course, has a whole genre of devoted to pickups and their drivers: Jerry Jeff Walker's "Pickup Truck Song," Brad Paisley's "Mud on the Tires" Trace Adkins' "Rough and Ready" (*gun rack, ball cap; don't take no crap*) and Joe Diffie's "Pickup Man," to pluck a few from a crowded field.

Insure.com conducted a poll recently and reported that women say men who drive trucks are the most attractive. And they were quite specific about it: A black pickup is best. They went even further: Black Ford pickups make men the most attractive they can be. So I guess a new Ford King Ranch Edition in black would be the perfect driving prescription for Texas men wanting to spiff up their image. Suggested that to my wife, and she said, "Yeah? Well, you can't have one. If you want another truck you can fix up that white '66 Chevy truck on blocks in your brother Redneck Dave's back yard."

I guess she hasn't seen any country music videos lately.

WHEN DAIRY QUEEN WAS FACEBOOK

Texas Monthly reported in 1979 that McDonald's was struggling to get a foothold in small-town Texas because the Dairy Queen was the social, cultural and culinary center of many a town.

The magazine interviewed James Utley, who shared franchises on 38 Dairy Queens in West Texas and wasn't worried about his Yankee chain competition:

"I don't think they can ever compete with a lady behind the counter who knows everybody's first name and has been pouring the town coffee for 10 or 20 years," he said.

Dairy Queen has been a Texas staple since before Whataburger. It's not a Texas company, though. The first Dairy Queen was opened in Joliet, Ill., in 1940. But Texas was not slow to embrace Dairy Queen as its own. *The Houston Chronicle* tells us that Dairy Queen sold its Texas territorial franchise rights around 1947, to Rolly Klose of San Antonio. These days, the oldest continually operating Dairy Queen in Texas is in Henderson, in northeast Texas. It opened in 1950.

Nowadays Texas has more DQ franchises than any other state — close to 600, according to the *Chronicle*. That's a lot of BeltBusters, y'all.

Texas Dairy Queens have long had their own Texas menu. They were serving burgers when the rest of the country's DQs were just selling soft-serve ice cream. The savory items still account for a larger portion of the Texas stores' sales.

DQs are among the most important institutions in small towns, right up there with school and church. It is often one of the few places to eat and the primary meeting place in town. Bankers go there for coffee before the bank opens; ranchers meet for lunch at DQ to discuss beef prices; teens go there after school to see each other seeing other.

Before the internet, the Dairy Queen served as Facebook. Status updates were shared in person, over coffee or by splitting a butterscotch sundae.

If someone were "in a new relationship," it was announced nonverbally when Becky Sue walked into the DQ on Jim Bob's arm, wearing his football letter jacket — or when Jim Bob drove up to one of the carhop-service spots and Becky Sue was scooted over all the way next to him on the car seat. When Becky Sue broke up with Jim Bob two months later, that too was announced when she arrived at DQ without Jim Bob and without his jacket. Change in relationship: formally announced.

No one took pictures of their food. They simply looked over to the nearby booth and said, "I like what Carlos is havin'."

Selfies were unheard of, and would have been regarded as immodest, anyway. But you could have someone else take a Polaroid snapshot of you getting your 4H Best of Breed Trophy, and the DQ people would post that on the bulletin board for all to see, next to snaps of newborns and newlyweds.

DQs don't have as dominant a social role as they once did, but they still serve as the pit-stop parking lot for kids cruising the new version of "the drag" on weekends.

And DQ has gone international. You can go to DQ in London or Madrid. You can even go to DQ in Thailand, where you can get a vanilla cone, but you can't get Texas Tacos.

WHATABURGER

What's the best Whataburger you ever had?

That's a question a friend of mine likes to ask everybody. Seems a strange question, but in Texas it isn't, necessarily. When he first asked me, I told him I could not tell him about the best Whataburger I ever had until I told him about the time I most wanted one.

Photo courtesy of Whataburger

Many years ago I took a job in Africa for a year. I just couldn't find much to eat there that I liked. I lost about 20 pounds in six months. I was so thin the local Care guys joked that that they might have to send me a package.

It was at this point of mild starvation that a friend back in Texas, Don Love, sent me a 2-by-3-foot poster of a Whataburger. Ten times life-size. Hot cheese, mustard and onions cascading seductively down the sides. Food porn. That is what it was.

I think it was the cruelest thing my former friend could have done. There I was in Whataburger-less Africa, staring at that poster every day. He had me Whataburger dreaming for months.

After a year in the African hinterlands, I flew back into DFW. Though it was midnight, I hailed a taxi and said, "Take me to the nearest Whataburger." I got a double-meat double-cheese burger, with extra tomatoes and chopped jalapenos. I Whatasized the fries and the Coke and chased it all with a chocolate shake and an apple pie.

Now that was the best Whataburger — indeed, the best meal — I ever had.

Photo courtesy of Whataburger

A replica of the first Whataburger, opened in Corpus Christi in 1950.

I am not alone in having such priorities. Soldiers on leave from posts around the world often go straight to Whataburger when they get home to Texas. I tell you, if the Pentagon could make MRE Whataburgers, they would lift morale.

Some people who live in Whataburger-less states will drive a couple of days to get a Whataburger. They don't even check into a hotel. They just eat one, take one to go and drive back home. So you see, there are only two kinds of states in America — those that have Whataburger and those that wish they did.

In the Whataburger states there are connoisseurs who will single a special Whataburger location that makes the best Whataburger of all. They will drive 60 or 70 miles in this Holy Grail quest to get what they feel is the Whataburger of Whataburgers.

Whataburger is a Texan chain, born on Ayers Street in Corpus Christi back in 1950. It was the brainchild of a burger visionary named Harmon Dobson. Dobson´s goal was simple: In a time of small burgers, he wanted to make one so big it would take two hands to hold it and so good that with one bite people would say, "What a burger!"

And it was so. Whenever my mom used to take my two brothers and me to Whataburger when we were just little boys, she would first spread newspapers across our laps in the back seat of our cavernous old Buick sedan. Then she would cut the burgers in half and serve them to us that way, so we wouldn't make a mess of her protective plastic seat covers.

Three things I loved about the early Whataburgers: 1. The triangular buildings that looked like the orange order cards everybody takes as souvenirs today. 2. The smell of beef patties and onions that permeated the air within half a block. 3. My mother saying, "If you finish all of that, you can have a shake."

I like that Whataburger is so well known that Google doesn't highlight the word as misspelled.

Today there are more than 800 Whataburger stores across the Orange States of Whataburger Nation, from Arizona to Florida. Texas remains the capital, of course. And all these Whataburgers are open 24 hours a day — proving every day that everything is bigger and better in Texas.

BLUE BELL ICE CREAM

They say that Texans who live outside of Texas — Texpatriates, I call them — long for three things most: Whataburger, Tex-Mex food and Blue Bell Ice Cream.

Blue Bell is an old Texas brand launched back in 1907. It has always promoted itself as "the little creamery in Brenham." Small and homey has been its cultivated image, as illustrated beautifully by its slogan: "We eat all we can and we sell the rest."

By 2015, though, Blue Bell was actually the third-largest ice cream company in America, behind Nestle's and Unilever, even though its products were available only in 23 states. Blue Bell's customer base was just that fanatically loyal. Then, that year, came the listeria scandal.

Blue Bell's legendary reputation for quality control was shattered. Ten people in four states were believed to be have been affected, dating all the way back to 2010. Three died. It was tragic for the families that lost loved ones, or suffered with them as they struggled to get well, and it was catastrophic news for the once-trusted brand that some experts feared might not survive the tragedy.

Blue Bell initially withdrew only part of its product line. As more cases were linked to Blue Bell products, and the cases were traced to both the Brenham plant and one in Oklahoma, the company finally recalled everything in April of 2015. Containers were cleared from the shelves of grocery-store and convenience-store freezers — 8 million gallons of ice cream and every single specialty product Blue Bell produced. The plants in Brenham, Oklahoma and Alabama would have to be shut down to undergo an extensive overhaul. Blue Bell execs laid off or furloughed thousands of employees in three states. For a company that had just hit record numbers in sales, the recall was a raw dose of reality.

Customers mourned. Thousands of photos were posted on social media showing people saddened by the empty freezers, some pretending to weep. On the notices of the recall that were posted on the freezer doors, customers penned love notes: "We love you Blue Bell," "Don't leave me, Blue Bell," "I have never wanted ice cream so bad," "God bless Blue Bell!"

A common meme on social media at that time was this: "Let me break this down for Northerners who can't understand the tragedy of recent events. The Blue Bell recall doesn't mean we're down a brand of ice cream. We don't BUY other brands of ice cream. The Blue Bell recall means WE ARE OUT OF

ICE CREAM!" After the shock of the recall and shutdown, a page on Facebook called "I love and support Blue Bell Ice Cream" was created, drawing a big following. T-shirts popped up that said, "I survived the Blue Bell famine of 2015." Some didn't wait until the recall was over, fearlessly buying half-gallons of Blue Bell on Craig's List for surprising sums.

All the love that was sent Blue Bell's way during the crisis didn't solve the company's problems. Blue Bell was in dire straits. Banks were not exactly lining up to bail the company out. Many business experts expected it would file for bankruptcy and be bought out by Nestle's or some other huge conglomerate.

Blue Bell needed a miracle, and a miracle came along. A white knight by the name of Sid Bass came to the rescue. He cut a check to Blue Bell for $125 million. It wasn't a gift; it was characterized both as a "loan" and an "investment," one that was figured would give Bass a nice stake in the company. But it was still a beautiful moment, because one Texas icon rode in to save another.

Sid Bass, if you don't know, is the eldest of the famous Bass brothers, all four of them billionaires from Fort Worth. The start of their fortunes came from their famous uncle, Sid Richardson, who was one of Texas' legendary oilmen from the last century. He was known in the '50s to be one of the richest men in America, and he established the Sid Richardson Foundation to support nonprofit organizations serving the people of Texas. You can't set foot on any university in Texas, it seems, without seeing the Sid Richardson theater, or art museum, or research center; you'll see the Bass name, as well, on many a cultural building around the state.

Doug Renfro, president of Renfro Foods in Fort Worth, told the *Fort Worth Star-Telegram* as the seven-month recall was coming to a close: "For Bass, who will always be the shrewd businessman, it must still be cool to be considered the white knight, the hero riding in to save a Texan icon."

When Bass' rescue was announced, social media erupted with applause and praise. You would see comments like "All hail Sid Bass" and "Someone needs to kiss him full on the lips and say thank you for Texas."

It all seems to be working out. As of 2018, Blue Bell had rebounded to the position of fifth-largest ice cream company in America. Its top-selling flavor, accounting for about 60 percent of sales, is still the much-loved Homemade Vanilla Ice Cream. I think I'll go get some now to go with the apple pie that's about to come out of the oven. Thank you, Sid, for making this moment possible.

FALFURRIAS BUTTER

Texas is home to a number of nationally and internationally famous brands, including Blue Bell Ice Cream, Southwest Airlines, Texas Instruments, Lone Star Beer, Dell, Imperial Sugar and the King Ranch.

Now, the King Ranch is a brand that came, quite literally, from a brand. The King Ranch even has its own brand of Ford pickup. And the King Ranch also figures in the history of another venerable Texas brand, Falfurrias Butter.

The story is a little circuitous, but here's a condensed version of the connection: In 1895, Richard King's partner in the original Santa Gertrudis Ranch, Mifflin Kenedy, sold 7000 cows to rancher Ed Lasater. These became the basis of Lasater's cattle-breeding empire. (Some 35 years later, by the way, the King Ranch bought 108,000 acres from Lasater, along a great number of cattle, to create the Encino Division of the King Ranch.)

People have wondered whether the butter is named for the town or the town for the butter, but they were actually both named after Lasater's ranch, which was named for a grove of trees called *La Mota de Falfurrias*. Lasater is reported to have claimed that that unique word, "Falfurrias," came from the Lipan Apache language and, loosely translated, meant "Land of Heart's Delight."

He founded the town in 1904, subdividing some of his ranch acreage for sale to farmers and settlers. Some five years later, Lasater's Falfurrias Creamery began producing Falfurrias butter from the herd of Jersey cows Lasater had become known for.

The butter was certainly the town's best-known export in those early days, and it likely remains so today (even though — spoiler alert — it is not actually made in Falfurrias any more).

Even the school mascot — the Falfurrias Jerseys — was named after the butter's real creators, the Jersey cows. Indeed, at one point Falfurrias was home to the largest Jersey cattle herd in the world.

And so that gave special meaning to the once popular bumper sticker there: "Watch Your Step — You're in Jersey Country."

Falfurrias butter remains a popular niche brand of butter. In Texas, it is sold at all the major grocery stores and some smaller ones, too. It has been quite popular in northern Mexico for generations, and the packaging is labeled in both Spanish and English.

A friend tells me that as a child in Saltillo he remembers his mother bringing back the *mantequilla dulce* (sweet butter) *de Falfurrias* as a special treat for the kids anytime she traveled to Texas.

I remember my father telling me a story that was common lore in Falfurrias: As a Texas Marine in World War was wading ashore in the battle for Okinawa, a Falfurrias Butter crate bumped up against his leg in the surf. He found it comforting, an assurance from home that all would be well. As Falfurrias Butter had military contracts, we accepted the story as truth, figuring the crate could have fallen from a Navy ship.

Falfurrias' heyday was in the '20s, when it was sold "all the way to the East Coast," Ed Lasater's grandson and namesake told a reporter for the *Dallas*

Observer a few years ago; after World War II, he said, the company restricted its market to Texas. Eventually, in the 1990s, the family sold the dairy; it has changed hands a few times since then but is now owned by the giant dairy cooperative Dairy Farmers of America, which also makes Borden's and Breakstone's products.

Rest assured, however, that Falfurrias Butter is still made in Texas — at ADF's huge Keller's Creamery plant in Winnsboro, east of Dallas.

When you drive through Falfurrias today, on Texas Highway 285, you can still see the vintage Falfurrias Butter sign on the side of the old Creamery Building. The town newspaper, *Falfurrias Facts*, occupies the building today.

In the interest of full disclosure and ethical transparency, I have to reveal that I am also an export of Falfurrias, and even though I know on which side my bread is buttered, so to speak, I assure you that it does not affect the veracity of this commentary.

DR PEPPER: A BIOGRAPHY

My favorite snack as a teenager was a Dr Pepper spiked with salty peanuts. You could do it with Coke, too, but to me Dr Pepper was clearly superior.

Photo by Carol M. Highsmith, Lyda Hill Texas Collection

You remember: You pour the peanuts into the Dr Pepper and let them float around and season the drink, then swig the soda and eat the peanuts as they slide down through the bottle's neck. Didn't get much better than that.

Dr Pepper has a pretty good claim — though it's disputed by Vernors — to being the oldest major soft drink that's still under production in America. It's older than Coca-Cola by a year.

It was created in 1885 by a pharmacist, Charles Alderton, in Waco, Texas.

He began serving it there at the soda fountain at Morrison's Old Corner Drug Store, and patrons originally called the pharmacist's blend of fruit syrups a "Waco," according to the Dr Pepper Museum. Customers would sit down on one of those old spinning stools and say, "Shoot me a Waco."

The unusual drink was an instant hit. As its popularity exploded, other local soda fountains began buying the syrup blend from Morrison's. Alderton and store owner Wade Morrison couldn't keep up with the demand, so Morrison and a partner founded a company to develop it as a soft drink. And a new name was created.

The name "Dr. Pepper" (the period was dropped in the '50s) is credited to Morrison. The most commonly repeated story is that Morrison named it after a doctor he had once worked for back in Virginia whose comely daughter had taken his fancy. The Dr Pepper Museum, however, doesn't give that story any more credence than the dozen or so others it says it has collected over the years.

Dr Pepper was already a regional success by the time of the 1904 World's Fair; as with so many other American pop-culture food classics, the fair's popularity launched it onto a national stage.

Maybe the unluckiest person in this whole affair was Charles Alderton, the pharmacist who created Dr Pepper. He simply gave away the recipe, evidently, because he was more interested in medicine than marketing.

These days, Dr Pepper's formula is held under stout security in a vault in the company's Plano headquarters, according to *Texas Monthly,* with backups in two separate bank vaults in the Dallas Fort Worth Metroplex.

Contrary to soda-pop mythology, Dr Pepper is not made of prune juice, according to both the Dr Pepper website and a brochure put out by the company to debunk this persistent rumor. "There are 23 flavors and other ingredients (none of which are prunes) that produce the inimitable taste of Dr Pepper," according to the brochure.

But the unique blend of flavors, along with the peppy carbonation, has garnered many die-hard fans. Many people swear that Diet Dr Pepper is the most un-diet-tasting diet soft drink in existence. And let's not forget Dublin Dr Pepper, now sadly out of production, but once regarded as the finest Pepper of all, thanks to the use of Imperial pure cane sugar.

A little side note: The numbers 10, 2, and 4 used to appear on every Dr Pepper bottle cap, in clock-face fashion, tying into the '50s Dr Pepper marketing slogan urging folks to take Dr Pepper breaks to pep them up at "10, 2 and 4 o'clock" — the times when energies often flag. That's the source of the mutant poker game called Dr Pepper, in which tens, twos and fours are wild.

A poker purist will not play Dr Pepper, but I like it. It is the only game in which I've ever held four of a kind.

THE AIRLINE DESIGNED ON A NAPKIN

This story starts off like many good stories do: Two men walked into a bar.

Now we have to expand it a little: Two men walked into a bar in San Antonio, some 50 years ago. Okay, it was actually a restaurant/bar. They ordered drinks. One grabbed a cocktail napkin, took out his pen and said to the other: "Here's the plan."

He drew a simple triangle on the napkin. At the apex of the triangle he wrote "Dallas." The bottom left he labeled "San Antonio." On the bottom right he wrote "Houston."

"There," he said. "That's the business plan. Fly between these cities several times a day, every day." And that is the story of how Southwest Airlines began — on a simple napkin in a bar in San Antonio.

The two men were Rollin King and Herb Kelleher. Rollin was a pilot and businessman; Herb was a lawyer. Rollin would become a managing director of the company, and Herb would become its chairman. There is a plaque at the Southwest Airlines headquarters that enshrines a version of the original napkin with this exchange: "Herb, let's start an airline." "Rollin, you're crazy. Let's do it!"

It's a good thing King was a lawyer, because he and Kelleher faced fierce legal opposition from several of the major airlines that didn't want the competition. It took until 1971, but they got their airline off the ground.

There are many things that Southwest became famous for: its LUV airlines nickname, still its stock-market trading symbol; calling its territory the Love Triangle and its hostesses (as they called flight attendants then) Love Hostesses. Southwest dressed them in hot pants and white go-go boots.

After all, they were competing in the sexy skies, where Braniff stewardesses wore uniforms designed by Emilio Pucci — including one collection, called the "Air Strip" collection, designed so that parts of the outfits would be removed as the flight progressed. Continental, another fierce competitor, advertised in a not-so-subtle double entendre, that "we really move our tail for you." Southwest fought back with ads in which hostesses cooed its new slogan, "there's somebody else up there who loves you."

But, beyond the sizzle, there was genuine business genius in Southwest's efficiencies — the peanut fares and the 10-minute turnaround (to get the plane unloaded, cleaned, restocked and ready for the next flight, which had never been achieved before). To date, Southwest has never recorded a fatality on any of its flights. Now that's a safety record!

Perhaps the coolest story in Southwest Airlines' history was the fare war it fought with now-defunct Braniff Airlines in 1972. Braniff went head-to-head with Southwest on the Houston-Dallas route, offering $13 one-way fares as a means of "breaking" Southwest, which didn't have the deep pockets the big guys like Braniff did.

Southwest responded with a $13 fare — or a full-price $26 fare that included a free fifth of premium liquor. The liquor would have cost less than $13 at retail, but business people booked Southwest on their company expense accounts and went home with a free bottle of their favorite liquor, sometimes two or three a week, stocking their bars very nicely courtesy of Southwest. According to airline lore, for two months, until Braniff surrendered, Southwest was Texas' biggest distributor of Chivas, Crown Royal and Smirnoff.

Deborah P. Franklin, left, and Karen Long, from the first Southwest Airlines flight atten-dant class in 1971.

In 2007, seven years before his death, Rollin King confessed to the *Dallas Morning News* that the napkin story wasn't entirely true — it was just a hell of a good story. It was too late, though: The myth had become more powerful than the reality. It had worked its magic over the years and could not be undone.

An old saying in marketing is that, when the legend becomes fact, print the legend. This is what I prefer to do. After all, it is hard to imagine that a concept so perfectly observant of the principle of Occam's Razor — that the simplest solution is the best — would not have at some point been sketched out on a napkin, a legal pad or the collected dust on the hood of Cadillac.

CHANGING TIMES

THINGS ARE DIFFERENT NOW IN TEXAS

Things are different in now in Texas. When I was a kid, I had to go inside to make a call. Now I often have to go outside to make one. They call this progress?

In my childhood we had one phone on the wall that we all ran to answer, just to find out who was calling. Now we all have our own phones, and we know who is calling before we don't answer it.

We used to stay in the truck to get gas and go inside to eat. Now it is the reverse. We get out to pump our gas and go through the drive-through for food.

Kids once drank out of the hose or the outside faucet, and now they run from that classic summer experience — right on inside for bottled water.

Only one in five of us is rural anymore, though many city people do try to hold on to a little farm or ranchito for weekends.

The small farmer is disappearing, being replaced by the monstrous commercial farms where tractors never sleep. Even small farmers today are likely to use GPS and long-range weather forecasting, something their grandfathers would have considered blasphemy. As one old farmer I once knew would say, "Don't watch the weather, man; watch the animals. They'll tell you what's comin.'"

Gas was once 35 cents a gallon, and someone else pumped it and washed your windshield and vacuumed the truck, too. Air and water were free. Now it's a dollar for air. A dollar for good Texas air! I never even expected to *pay* for a drink of water, much less to pay for *air*? That is beyond anything I ever would have thought possible.

Sundays were quiet back then. All shut down. Everything except movie theaters and a few restaurants were closed to allow for church attendance. Blue laws, they were called. Those are gone. The Blue Light Special took their place.

Most food was cooked and eaten at home. Eating out was rare. Now lots of folks I know eat out most every meal.

Dinner was at noon. The evening meal was supper.

One TV per house. Now there are TVs in every room. Sometimes two to a room, competing with each other. We had three channels on TV. Now 300 and nothin' on.

Today teenagers are happier cruising the net than cruising round town. Having too many windows open means something quite different today.

We have more drugstore cowboys than real ones. And roundups are done with helicopters instead of horses.

Cowboy trucks used to be beat-up four-wheel-drive off-road trucks. Now urban cowboys have shiny four-wheel drives whose massive tires have barely touched anything but pavement.

Yes, things are different now. But I will certainly embrace one element of progress wholeheartedly: air conditioning, perfected appropriately in Houston. In the old days we just sweated all the time. Now we are cool most everywhere if we want to be. And even the word "cool" is still cool. Never went out of style.

And, yes, I like that the movie theaters have more than one movie a week. I like the democratization of information and the amazing amount of choice that exists in the world. I am happy for the advances in medicine and the efforts to beat back, over time, many of the isms — racism, sexism, ageism, ethnocentrism. Unfortunately, unbridled narcissism is healthier than ever, as common as tumbleweeds in Terlingua and spikes on a horned frog.

WORDS, THEY ARE A-CHANGIN'

Slang is the working class of words. The American poet Carl Sandburg once said, "Slang is a language that rolls up its sleeves, spits on its hands and goes to work."

But slang is always changing. For an older guy like me, it's hard to keep up with. The slang of old-time or traditional Texas is quite familiar to me. Those of my generation, even though we live in cities, still use farm and ranch expressions like "all hat and no cattle" and "a tough row to hoe." We find it hard to escape Texas's agrarian past. The language holds on, and it's hard to teach an old dog new linguistic tricks.

But teenagers in Texas nowadays seem to be more influenced by the national youth culture than by what we think of as traditional agrarian Texas culture. Oh, yes, many still say "fixin' to and "y'all," but those are often the only tip of the hat they give to classic Texas expressions.

Lately I've been collecting some examples of the words that seem to be currently in vogue but that may well fall out of common use by the time this is published.

Did you know that "on fleek," "squad," and "lit" are on their way out? Neither did I. Those words are going out before I knew they were in. Hell, I just learned "hipster" a few months ago, which likely proves I'm not one. It also shows I'm late to learn new slang. No surprises there. By the time I catch up with a new movement, it has generally moved on.

Millennials, by contrast, change slang faster than Taylor Swift changes boyfriends.

One trend that I have noticed lately is how many words or expressions that were common 20 years ago have either disappeared altogether or have had their meanings reversed.

"Parking" is a case in point. Forty years ago, parking was the term for finding a quiet spot on a country road and enjoying some intimate time with your date.

That meaning is gone. If you bring up that term in front of today's college students, they will say, "I know. The parking problem on campus is terrible." If you explain what it used to mean they will say, "Oh, you mean Netflix and chill!" Or "hooking up."

"Shade" is something I've always tried to sit in. Now, evidently, it is something you can throw. At someone else, to let them know they are beneath you.

"Sick" is the new cool. "Sick" used to mean ill, but now it is high praise: "That's a sick tune you´re playin." Wicked is also strangely good. "Leah, you're sick and wicked." That's a compliment!

"Savage" used to be a word no one wanted to be associated with. Now it works as praise. "That motorcycle jump was savage, dude." Or you can use it as a verb: "You savaged that Snickers bar."

"Dope" used to be a fool or an idiot or someone ignorant — as in, "He's a dope." Now it's something or someone who is super-cool, as in, "That's so dope," or "Nobody's dope as me."

"Howdy" has largely been replaced, at least among some millennials, by " 'Sup," a contraction of "What's up?"

"Awesome" has changed in the sense that it used to be a powerful word, a word that could bench-press 500 pounds. It was reserved for godly things, for divine things, for things inspiring awe. You would use it for a crimson sunset over El Capitan in West Texas. But now this sublime word is used promiscuously — as in, "Those are awesome tacos" or "You'll be here in 10 minutes? Awesome." Inflation has set in. "Awesome" has lost its awesomeness. The same is true for "amazing."

We have some nonverbal reversals, too. Wearing your cap backwards or sideways used to be considered nerdy. Wearing it cocked to the side once made you seem like a clown. Today, wearing it that way can be "dope." But only in youth culture. If I were to do it, I would look like an old clown. Best for me to stick to Stetsons.

Used to be that wearing your shirttail out was slovenly. Now it's stylish.

Wearing your shirt tucked in is considered nerdy. Out is in and in is out. Unless you are talking about Western fashion, where the tucked tradition mostly prevails.

One word that seems to have weathered the decades without changing is "cool." Cool is so cool it can use itself to define itself. "Cool" was cool in the '60s, and it is still cool today. Not only is it cross-generational, it is cross-cultural, too. "Cool" is cool in the African-American world. It's cool in the Hispanic world, and it's cool in Anglo culture, too. It's cool in rap and it's cool in country. And it is transcontinental as well. People around the world who don't speak English seem to know at least two words: "OK" and "cool." "Cool" is singularly diverse, with diverse acceptance. And that's awesome.

Not long ago, a younger, determinedly on-fleek friend heard me making these observations. His response: "Don't be throwin' shade on our slang. You just need to get woke, dude."

That's probably true. Workin' on it.

YOLO, y'all.

RAISING BOYS

A great many things have changed in Texas since I was a boy, and one of the greatest changes is in father-son relationships.

When I was a boy, my father knew more than I did, and I knew he knew more than I did. If my bicycle chain came off, or the bike got a flat, I would take it to Dad and he would pop the chain back on with a screwdriver, oil it down with WD-40 or patch the tube, all in a five-minute pit stop. He would roll the bike back to me, tousle my hair and say, "There you go." If my BB gun got jammed he would pop it open, remove the stuck BB and hand my BB gun back, saying, "There you go, son, locked and loaded."

Now that I have boys myself I find that I don't have much expertise in their world. I cannot solve their technical problems. They say things like, "Dad, my Xbox isn't properly interfacing with the Call of Duty server at Microsoft." Or, "Dad, can you download the synchronization patch for my Wizard program?"

All I can do is look at them and say, "How's your bicycle, son? How's your BB gun doin'?"

When I was a boy, you couldn't get me inside; now I can't get them outside.

My boyhood wars were fought outside on a battlefield that was five acres of backyards. We fought with dirt clods and oranges and sometimes BB guns, if we had on thick winter coats.

My sons' wars are fought on a 32-inch, two-dimensional screen in a dark room. All you see in there is flickering light when you walk by. I tell my sons that mankind went through thousands of years of evolution to escape the cave, and now they have moved back into one.

I suppose every father thinks his childhood was purer or tougher than his son's.

Just a few Christmases ago I stood with my father and grandfather watching my son play with a remote-controlled robot dinosaur.

I remarked that my son's toys were incredibly advanced, almost like something out of science fiction.

"When I was a boy," I said, "advanced technology was an electric train."

My dad said, "In my day we only had rusty old metal trucks that we pushed around outside in the dirt."

My grandfather said, "Hell, in my day we had to *pretend* we had toys."

A TALE OF TWO TEXASES: 1918 AND 2118

In my last broadcast of 2017, I decided to look back 100 years, at 1918, and forward 100 years, to make some guesses about 2118 in Texas.

In 1918 there were fewer than 250,000 vehicles on the road in Texas. No driver's license was required to pilot one, by the way. Given that there were only about 5 million of us back then, we had roughly one vehicle for every 20 people. That made getting to the family reunion a tight squeeze.

Today there are 22 million vehicles on the road in Texas (sometimes I think all of them are in the I-35 corridor, or Central Expressway or the Gulf Freeway). There are 28 million Texans. Subtract the children and you have damn near one vehicle for every Texan of driving age. Since 1918, cars and trucks have proliferated far faster than Texans. We've seen a twenty-fold increase in vehicles and only a sixfold increase in people. We're adding cars and trucks faster than we're making Texans.

In 1918 we had more people than California, about 25 percent more. By 2018 California was beating *us* by a bit more than 25 percent; Texas, 27 million; California, 40 million. Of course, at the rate Californians are moving here, this may soon reverse itself.

Two worldwide events overshadowed all else in the year 1918. One was the ending of World War I. (Incidentally, it was called "the Great War" then. It didn't become World War I until we had a World War II, which created the need for the distinguishing labeling.) A million Texans registered for the draft, and 200,000 of them fought in the Great War. Texas volunteerism was high, perhaps because Germany had offered Mexico a deal in a communique called the Zimmermann Telegram: If Mexico threw in with Germany, Germany would help Mexico get Texas (and what's now New Mexico and Arizona) back.

Some 5200 Texas servicemen (and women) died during the war years. About a third of them died not overseas but in the United States — many of them from the other devastating event that struck in 1918, the influenza pandemic, better known as the Spanish flu. It was particularly sad that we had soldiers survive four years of unholy trench warfare and mustard gas only to come home to die of the flu.

The Spanish flu was unusual in that 20-to-40-year-old adults were most at risk rather than children and old people. The pandemic was to grip the world for some two years. The virus struck suddenly and could kill quickly.

Children who survived the flu that year, some believe, went on to live healthy lives because they developed powerful immunities. My mother had the Spanish flu when she was 8. She lived to be almost 102. She was in good company: Walt Disney had it, Woodrow Wilson had it; so did Texas-born novelist Katherine Anne Porter, who later wrote a novella based on the epidemic, *Pale Horse, Pale Rider*. A study by Vanderbilt University in 2008 found that people like those survivors still had the Spanish flu antibodies working hard in their bodies 90 years after they had it.

World War I touched many, but the flu affected many more. Worldwide, far more people died of the Spanish flu than died in World War I. Texas cities with military bases, like El Paso, were particularly hard-hit. Some 600 people died in El Paso, almost 1 percent of the population; thousands more, of course, had it and survived.

Today we have flu vaccines, first produced by Jonas Salk and Thomas Francis in 1938. So, though a pandemic on the scale of the 1918 scourge is not impossible, most experts feel it is highly unlikely. We cannot necessarily say the same for world wars, however.

Turning to the future, what will Texas look like in 100 years, in 2118? All one can do is look at trends and guess. As noted business theorist Peter Drucker said, "Trying to predict the future is like trying to drive down a country road at night with no lights on while looking out the back window." With that warning, let's try anyway.

If we go by the futurists at Google, we can predict that there will be fewer cars on the road per capita than now. Self-driving buses and cars are already on the horizon. Some of the future-casters believe we will simply hail self-driving ride services using some future version of smartphones that probably won't be called phones anymore. I wonder if we will have taxi pick-ups, nicely lifted, with the occasional set of longhorns strapped to the front, just for nostalgia.

In 2017, I asked Texas' official demographer, Steve Murdock — everybody's go-to guy for the future of Texas — what he thought the Texas population would look like in 2118. His response:

"If Texas continues to grow as it has in the recent past, one would expect it to increase its population to more than 80 million by 2118. This assumes that Texas will obtain technology and other factors to increase the water supply."

That would put us in the neighborhood of present-day Egypt for size and population.

By 2050 or 2060, Murdock predicts, Texas will be about 55 percent Hispanic and 20 percent Anglo, but he won't venture much beyond that in any trend predictions. He did warn, however, that Texas needs very much to ensure educational opportunity for all, or we will not see the success in the century ahead that we enjoyed in the last one.

My personal guess is that Texas will be much more urban in 2118 than it is today, particularly east of I-35. DFW, Houston and San Antonio will be super-cities. Austin may well be a kind of giant suburb of San Antonio. We might see San Antonio and Houston fighting over city limit signs.

If the big tech giants have the future accurately envisioned, our cities will be more people-friendly, pushing vehicles out of our streets and reclaiming many of them as green spaces for walking and biking and sports. And we will all have AI robots.

I just hope they say "howdy" and "fixin' to" and "while I'm up, can I get y'all a beer?"

DOS MUNDOS

THE NEW IMMIGRANTS

This was the situation: The new immigrants to Texas were becoming quite a problem. They were coming across the river in droves. Some were legal and some were undocumented. Some were living on land they had legally acquired and some were squatters, living on land that belonged to others. The legal immigrants were being followed by family members who were arriving without proper papers. The government was frustrated and trying desperately to come up with a solution.

Many were good people, hard workers. But as a group they would mostly keep to themselves. They wouldn't assimilate. They wouldn't acculturate. They refused to learn the language. Most were of a different religion from that which was most common in their new country.

There was talk of posting the military all along the river. The borders and immigration laws needed to be enforced. The government passed a law prohibiting all new immigration to Texas from the neighboring republic. The military was in fact sent to ports of entry to turn back those without proper documents.

Sound familiar? These issues were being discussed in Texas almost 200 years ago.

The years I'm talking about here were the 1820s and early 1830s, before the battle of the Alamo, before the battle of San Jacinto.

The immigrants were not Mexican. They were Anglo Americans coming in from Louisiana, Arkansas, Tennessee and other Southern states. The river the immigrants were crossing was not the Rio Grande, but the Sabine, the border between Texas and Louisiana.

The concerned government was not in Austin, but in Mexico City. Texas, of course, belonged to Mexico at the time.

There were calls to put the Mexican Army on the eastern border. The Mexican authorities didn't do it, but they did place small military contingents at ports of entry along the coast.

The language the immigrants would not learn was Spanish. That was part of the deal: If they got cheap land, they agreed to become Mexican citizens and learn Spanish. Most reneged.

The religion they would not embrace was Catholicism, even though that was part of the deal, too. As Mexican citizens, they were supposed to become Catholic. Most did not. Priests lived among them, but there was little effort to enforce that requirement.

It is surprising to see how trends, in some ways, have reversed themselves over a couple of centuries. I'm not interested in getting into the high weeds of politics here. I'll leave the cautionary tales to others. But I do find this a good illustration of a clever adage that is often attributed to Mark Twain but whose real author remains a mystery:

"History may not repeat itself, but it does rhyme."

SPANISH FOR GRINGOS: AN INTRODUCTION

I suppose the first Spanish word I ever heard was *gringo*.

The second word I heard was *pinche*, which preceded *gringo* and was directed at me.

I wasn't offended. I was told by my boyhood friend Gonzalo that the speaker was complimenting my frugality.

As an Anglo Texan, I think it is a good idea to master what I like to call Spanish for Gringos. This is important as a means of fully enjoying the bicultural nature of Texas. Why be left out of half of our state's heritage?

With or without the *pinche* epithet, in addition to being called *gringos*, we are also called *bolillos,* which is because we are the color of those beautiful pointy-ended white-flour dinner rolls. Another fine compliment.

Most gringos know the word *cerveza*. That was the first word I learned in a bar. Followed by *bien fria*: Good and cold. *Otra.* Another. And, after a few *otras*, I needed this phrase: *"Donde esta el baño?"* Survival Spanish. Priceless.

Spanish is a diminutive language. Thanks to the diminutives -*ito* and -*ita*, everything is, affectionately, little. My wife will say, *"Quieres huevito y caféci-to?"* "Would you like a little egg and a little coffee?" I will say yes, and soon here she comes with three scrambled eggs wrapped in two large flour tortillas with chorizo sausage and a mug of coffee. And I wonder, "What happened to the -*ito*?"

Everything in Spanish is -*ito*. I know a guy named Carlos who weighs 300 pounds but his Mama still calls him *Carlitos*.

That is another thing gringos should know: Spanish is a contradictory language. Big is small and small is big. Go to any construction site and you will find an anorexic-looking man who is called *Gordo* (Fattie). You will find a dark-haired man called Blondie, or *Güerito*. Newlyweds call each other *viejo* and *vieja*, old man and old lady.

Consider that famous drink, the margarita. It is a drink that means little Margaret. But they bring it in a massive glass that could hold the Arctic Ocean.

Ahorita (somewhat like "directly" in Texan) doesn't mean "now." It means soon, which means possibly tomorrow, or next week.

Making sure the guest is well-fed is a central value of the Hispanic household. At 11 in the morning the hostess will ask if you would like something to eat. You will say, "I already had eggs and bacon and toast," and she will say, "*Pero, necesita un pedacito de pastel.*" You need a little piece of cake. "*Siéntate.*" Have a seat. And all you can do is surrender.

We gringos do not need a huge vocabulary or perfect pronunciation. We just need to try. You can say "*Quiero una cervezita, bien fria, por favor*" in the rawest East Texas redneck accent, and the Hispanic world will open to you because you are trying. They will toast you with "*Salucita!*"s and welcome you with *abrazotes* (big hugs). Unless they are tourists from Monterrey. Then you are still just a *pinche gringo*.

LINGO FOR GRINGOS:
TEN WORDS ALL TEXANS SHOULD KNOW

To further enhance your education in survival Spanish, I've put together a list of words I call "lingo for gringos." These are 10 Spanish words all gringos who live in Texas should know.

I'm not talking about the easy words like *cerveza* and *vino*, *tortilla*, *taco* and *baño*. And I'm not talking about the common words we say every day that are actually Spanish words: patio, plaza, armadillo, mosquito, etc. I've chosen 10 words that are commonly used in everyday conversations and that might be characterized as colloquialisms among Spanish-speakers of Mexican descent.

I've tried to give you a rough idea of how these words are pronounced, but you'll do better if you seek out one of the many sources of Spanish audio pronunciation online (look for the little speaker icon) and listen.

If you know very little Spanish but at least know these words, you will have a clue as to what is going on around you. *Listos*? Ready? Here we go.

1. *Aguas* (AHg-was). Uttered sharply, in an admonitory tone, it means "Watch out" or "Be careful." My wife uses it often when children are in danger: "*Aguas, aguas!*" she says with the same tone of impending doom, whether they are really about to walk off a cliff or merely about to get gently bumped by the fridge door. The expression has its roots in the cities of long ago when waste water, and worse, used to be tossed out the second-story windows and walkers below would warn their companions by yelling "*Aguas!*"

2. _Guácala_ (gWAH-ka-la) is a slang word, popular throughout Latin America. It means "gross" or "disgusting." It is also fun to say, because it has an onomatopoeic quality that makes the word sound like what it describes. It animates the moment: "Guácala" for all that disgusts you.

3. _Ni modo_ (KNEE moh-doh). It is two words, but it always sounds like one to me. I love this expression. It means "What can you do?" "It's out of our hands." "Whatever will be will be." It can also mean "No big deal" or "Whatever," depending on the speaker and the context, but mostly it is an expression of fatalism. "They've changed the computer system at work again." "_Ni modo._"

4. _N'ombre_ (NOME-bray). This is not the word that means "name," but a contraction that is short for "No, hombre." _N'ombre._ "No way." It has many nuances of meanings, but for the most part it expresses surprise, disbelief, or even shock and must be said accordingly, in a tone of disbelief. "Did you know Lisa and Chuy eloped?" "_N'ombre!_"

5. _Güey_ (pronounced like "way" with just a whisper of a hard g in front of it) is analogous to "dude" or "man" or "bro." "_N'ombre, güey!_" "It can't be, dude!" The Big Lebowski would be the ultimate _güey. El Güey aguanta:_ The Dude abides.

6. _Chisme_ (CHEESE-meh) is gossip or rumor. Good, juicy stories. "_Tienes chisme?_" "Got any good gossip?" When Facebook was new, I would hear people say, "Facebook _es puro chisme,_" — pure gossip — meaning that private information could easily slip out and travel to all the last places you would want it to go, like to your mother's page.

7. _Naca_ or _naco_ (NAH-ka, NAH-koh). Don't confuse this with _narcos_ — those who work for cartels. It means a person who sports unsophisticated tastes, or, at least, less sophisticated than yours. She or he is often, like true rednecks, proud of being authentic. If Jeff Foxworthy spoke Spanish, he might do this routine: "If you think Sharpie eyebrows are high-fashion, you might be a _naca._" And, if you think mullets are in — hate to say it — _N'ombre, que naco!_

8. _Sinvergüenza._ (seen-vair-gWEN-sa). Without shame. Without embarrassment. When someone stuffs her purse with buffet food at the reception, we say, with a distinct tut-tutting tone of disapproval, "_Sinvergüenza._"

9. Resaca. (reh-SOCK-ah). Hangover. A common word in the Rio Grande Valley, _resaca_ in its original usage refers to the oxbow lakes that are found there — former channels of the river that have silted up and become cut off from the main course of the river. Just as the oxbow lake is a leftover or hangover from the Rio Grande, _resaca_ is the name for a hangover from the tequila of the night before. "_Tengo una resaca horrible._" "I have a horrible hangover." _Cruda_ is more commonly used, but it is, compared to _resaca_, crude.

10. _Órale_ (OH-ra-leh, with the second syllable rhyming with "bad").

Órale is famous for having about 40 different meanings achieved by variations in vocal inflection and situation. Some linguists say it has 820 meanings depending on the tone, time of day, style of hair and what shoes you're wearing. It is used for enthusiastic affirmation. Someone says, "*Vamonos por una cerveza*," and you say, "*Órale*." It means "Let's go ahead," "Absolutely," "Let's do it," "Hurry up," "Wow," and dozens of other things. One Texas English equivalent for *órale* is simply, "There you go."

So there you have your 10 indispensable words. I want to say *gracias* to my gorgeous wife Lupita, who has taught me these words and many others I cannot share here. But these 10 will serve you well in navigating our increasingly multilingual world.

— *Soy W. F. Fuerte, "Estos son Cuentos de Tejas: Algunos son Cierto"*
— *Co-written by Lupita Strong*

DRIVING IN MEXICO: EN LA FRONTERA

Driving in Mexico used to be a favorite pastime of mine. I used to drive all over that country, by myself, and I found nothing but kindness for a stranger. Much of the country I enjoyed as an eco-tourist: monarch butterfly migrations, mesmerizing rain forests, exotic tropical birds. Now, when I go, which is rarely, I am more like a *narco*-tourist — risking my life at every turn, especially along the *frontera*. I like that they call it the *frontera*, the frontier, what they used to call the Wild West in Texas. These days it is appropriately named.

As soon as many Mexicans cross the river going back home from vacations in Texas, they take off their seat belts. They are free. Seat belts are required by law in Mexico, but the law is not much enforced. In fact, most of Mexico's traffic laws function more like suggestions than commands. There is a posted speed limit, but it is a suggestion of safe speed. If you see a sign that says "*NO ENTRE*," it really means, "It is best not to enter here, but if you must, then be careful."

Stop signs are for the one who is last to the intersection. I believe there are no defensive-driving courses in Mexico. I think they just offer offensive driving. It has always seemed odd to me that Mexico is a country where the people live slow but drive fast. They live at a leisurely, wonderfully civilized pace, but when they get behind the wheel everybody is Mario Andretti.

Then there are the *topes*. *Topes* are speed bumps. This is Mexico's favorite form of traffic control. I recently drove into Matamoros; while crossing the bridge and passing through customs, I patiently steered my Jeep diagonally over, and I kid you not, 33 *topes*. That was a foreshadowing of what the Mexican streets and roads offer in general.

There are two types of *topes*. The gentle rolling asphalt *tope* you can take at 20 miles an hour. And then there is the steel-reinforced concrete *tope* that will rattle your teeth at .2 mph. It was designed by Lego, I think. And I would not object to *topes* so much, except for their custom of putting the tope sign right by the tope. So you are driving down a nice quiet country road and all of sudden — TOPE!! They should just put *SORPRESA!* ("Surprise!") on the sign. It seems to pop up out of the pavement like something out of a child's music box.

And then there is this curiosity: You will often see a mechanic's shop only a hundred yards past the *tope*. This is good marketing, because it is about 100 yards past the *tope* that you realize your muffler is gone, and the only reason it is gone is because the transmission removed it when the *tope* tore through it. Location, location.

Glorietas, traffic circles, are also quite popular. They are complicated at rush hour. People have been known to disappear into them, never to be seen again.

Something I always appreciated about driving in Mexico is that if you ever do get stopped — which is rare, but more common if you are a big *gringo* with Texas plates — you can hold traffic court right by the road.

I was pulled over for allegedly exceeding the suggested speed limit. I asked if I could pay the fine right there. They said the fine was "50 dollars." I thought they meant pesos, but for my convenience they had already done the conversion.

So here is the great thing about this moment, if you understand the custom: The police are also judge and jury. You can plead your case right there at the side of the road.

So I told them I would pay $10. They said $40. I told them that I only had $20 on me and that was all I could pay. This plea for leniency went up to a higher court. The policeman and his partner are, together, the appeals court. They went off to the far side of the car to discuss my appeal for five minutes. I think they just did it for show and were really just discussing good places to have lunch. They came back and said $20 would be OK. So I paid and off I went.

What I particularly love about this kind of justice is that it is so efficient. The same infraction in Texas would have cost me much more money, $200, probably. And then I would have taken a hit on my insurance premiums, too. If I wanted to challenge it, I would have had to take a day off to go to court and plead my case in front of a judge. Very time-consuming. Of course, I could just admit my guilt and mail in the fine, but then I would have to find my checkbook (something I never use anymore) and then an envelope and then a pen, and God knows where a stamp is! And then I have to get it to the post office. Too many complications.

No, no. I prefer my traffic court held at the side of the road on a Mexican highway. Not only is it more efficient justice, it is less expensive justice, too.

CHICLE

"*Quieres Chicle?*" You want some gum? Anytime I walk across a bridge into Mexico, I am met by a swarm of kids saying, "*Oye, gringo, quieres Chicle?*" The Chiclet kids, I call them. The Chiclet mafia.

It is appropriate, one might say, to be met at the border with gum, since the American gum industry was launched by Mexico. And you won't believe who had a hand in the launching of it.

It all started with an unlikely connection between a New York photographer/inventor and a famous Mexican national. Their paths crossed around 1869, in New York, where the famous Mexican national had been exiled to Staten Island.

Thomas Adams was the inventor, a bit of a tinkerer. The exiled Mexican had an idea that *chicle*, the natural gum from the *sapodilla* tree that the Mayans had chewed for probably hundreds of years, could be vulcanized and used instead of, or in addition to, rubber — which was quite expensive — to make bicycle tires and other rubber-centric items. He needed money to fund his return to Mexico and to political power, and he just happened to be able to lay his hands on a large quantity of *chicle* from Mexico. Adams knew that if the idea worked they both could become quite rich.

Well, Adams tried every way he could to use *chicle* as a substitute or additive for rubber, but it wouldn't make a tire. What he did discover, however, was that the Mayans were right — it was fun to chew, and more supple than the paraffin-based chewing gums that were the norm then.

So he went to work cooking up and forming *chicle* into pieces of chewing gum to sell to drugstores and confectionary shops. "Adams New York Snapping and Stretching Gum" was launched. As his gum grew more popular, in 1871 Adams invented a machine to make the gum, which he flavored with mint, sugar and licorice. The hard-candy gum called Chiclets was added to the Adams line (which eventually was to become Adams Cadbury) in the early 1900s.

Adams' famous associate, as it turns out, had been quite wrong in thinking that *chicle* would make a good tire. He'd also, it could be said, displayed bad judgment by giving up and returning to Mexico before Adams had hit on the chewing-gum idea. But that wasn't the first thing he'd ever been wrong about. He was also wrong in thinking he could easily defeat 187 Texans at the Alamo. That cost him a third of his army. Antonio López de Santa Anna was also wrong to think he and the troops he led could take a siesta when Sam Houston was wide awake across the prairie at San Jacinto. That cost him Texas.

Only one thing went right for Santa Anna that day in 1836: He was able to escape the battle on horseback. He would almost certainly have been killed outright had he been captured during the battle, but the next day, when a party of scouts found him hiding in the grass and brought him back to camp, the Texas commander, Gen. Sam Houston, spared his life. Many of the angry Texas soldiers wanted to hang Santa Anna from a handy cottonwood tree, but Houston stopped them. Indeed, Santa Anna spoke later of the graciousness and kindness he had been shown by Houston, his triumphant enemy.

Historians, including Alamo Director of History and Curation Richard Bruce Winders, tell us that Santa Anna, as president of Mexico, was far more valuable to the Texans alive than dead. The captured president was required to sign the Treaties of Velasco, recognizing the independence of Texas, before he was released to Mexico.

Santa Anna survived his political catastrophe and political exile. He fought against the Americans in the Mexican-American war and lost. He fought against the French and lost his leg, but he compensated for the loss by burying his leg with full military honors. Truth is indeed stranger than fiction.

And almost as strange is the fact that Santa Anna eventually took refuge in New York, in the country against which he had once led armies, and there inadvertently launched the U.S. gum industry.

So, next time someone offers you a Chiclet, think of Sam Houston. Without him it might not exist.

HAPPY-HOUR HOMILIES

THE TEXAS RANCHER
AND THE NEW YORK BANKER

This story comes under the heading of folklore, a story that rises up out of the people and migrates and mutates. There is a New York version, a Jewish version, an Italian version, a Southern version and the Texas version, which goes like this:

A Texas rancher walks into a bank in New York City and asks for a $5000 loan for the period of a month.

The banker hesitates. He is uncertain about it because he thinks the Texan looks like a pure redneck, and, truth be told, rather poor. So he decides to blow him off quickly.

"Do you have any collateral to put up for the loan?" the banker says.

The rancher says, "Yep, got that Ford F-250 settin´ across the street there. Worth 70 thousand all decked out that way."

The banker rolls his eyes and says, "How much do you owe on that truck?"

"Not a dime," says the rancher. "All paid for."

The banker leans forward and changes his tune: "Well, sir, I don´t see why we couldn´t loan you $5000. We could go up to $40,000, if you would like, over a longer period, of course."

"Nope," says the rancher, "The $5000 will do. A month is all I need."

"Do you mind if I ask why you need the loan?" asks the banker.

The rancher says, "I drove up from my little ranch near Abilene to do some business here and suddenly got an unexpected opportunity, a bucket-list item, to fly over to España and maybe purchase an Andalusian horse, if I can afford it. Little cash-poor just now. Need some walkin'-around money."

"Well, this should be no problem," says the banker. "We can certainly help you out."

"Just one thing," says the rancher: "Can we skip puttin' a lien on the title? I reckon clearing a New York lien from a Texas title can be like herdin´ cats."

"I'll tell you what," says the banker. "Just leave the truck with us as hard collateral and pick it up when you come back."

The rancher thinks it over a minute and says, "Well, it´s a bit unusual, but

I guess it will be all right." He slides the keys across the desk to the banker.

In 10 minutes all the formalities are settled, the banker gives the rancher $5000 in cash, and the Texan is off to Spain.

One month later the rancher returns to the bank and pays the banker $5000 dollars, plus $28.22 for one month's interest.

The banker walks the rancher out to the front of the bank to wait for his truck to be brought down from the garage. As they are waiting he says, "Sir, while you were gone I ran a full credit check on you, just for the hell of it. I found that you are quite wealthy. You have a very large ranch, many head of cattle and oil and gas interests. You didn't really need this loan, did you?"

The rancher grins and replies, "No, sir, I didn't. Not really."

"Mind if I ask why you got it?" says the banker.

At this point the truck arrives from the bank's garage. The rancher hops in and powers down the window. He leans out toward the banker and says, "Where else was I gonna park a big ol' F-250 in New York City for a whole month for just 28 bucks?"

The rancher tips his hat. "Much obliged to you," he says as he pulls away from the curb.

THREE TEXAS PRIDE STORIES

I've been sad lately noticing how the oral tradition seems to be dying. Twenty years ago friends would often come up to me on the street and say, "Hey, I got a story for you." But now they just come up to me and hold out their phone and say, "Seen this?" and laugh. It's just not the same.

Today I thought I'd do what I can to fight this trend. I'm going tell you three short stories (or jokes) that showcase our Texas pride. You can even pass them on, if you think them worthy — just not on your phones.

The first one I heard from my father when I was about 10. It was my first exposure to this genre, and I was hooked. It went like this:

"A man from Kentucky was talking to a Texan and bragging about all the gold they had in Fort Knox. The Kentuckian said, "You know we have enough gold in Fort Knox to build a wall of solid gold, six-foot high, all the way around Texas?"

The Texan said, "Is that so? Tell you what, you go ahead and build your wall — and if we like it, we'll buy it."

Now that's not exactly roll-out-of-your-chair funny, but it was my first exposure to that kind of story, and I thought it was hugely clever. At 10, I'd had no idea such stories existed, and I was eager to hear more.

Here's another one:

This comes from John Gunther's book *Inside U.S.A.* You remember Gunther, who was famous for passing along the quote, "If a man's from Texas, he'll tell you. If he's not, why embarrass him by asking?"

Gunther writes that a man from Boston was visiting a friend in Texas. The Bostonian was tired from traveling and went to bed early. As he pulled back the blankets, he was shocked to find a 12-inch lobster waiting for him under the covers. Rather than let the Texan get the better of him with this practical joke, he picked up the lobster and took it into the living room where his friend was reading the paper.

He held up the lobster and said, "You sure do have big bedbugs in Texas."

The Texan peered up over the paper, squinted at the lobster and drawled, "Well, must be a young 'un."

The last story, truly a Texas classic from the '60s, concerns a prideful Texan who died and went to heaven. Saint Peter was giving him an orientation tour to get him acquainted with the beauties of the place.

He first showed off some snow-covered peaks reminiscent of the Swiss Alps, and the Texan said, "Well, they're nice, if you like your mountains all covered in snow that way. I like mine with a light dusting of snow now and then and otherwise hot and dry, like we have 'em in Big Bend."

Next Saint Peter took the Texan by the elbow and flew him up to a peak overlooking a sparkling mountain river.

"You ever seen a more beautiful blue than that?" Saint Peter queried.

"No," said the Texan, "but you want to see the most beautiful turquoise river ever, you need to see the Devils River in West Texas. Sorry to mention him, but that is the name of it. And don't get me started on the Guadalupe..."

Saint Peter interrupted him and pointed to the Alpine forest whose leaves were waving before them in the gentle mountain breeze.

Said the Texan: "Impressive, but nothing can steal my heart away from the Piney Woods of East Texas. You ever seen the Big Thicket?"

Exasperated, Saint Peter flew the Texan over to the very edge of heaven and had him look over the side. Far, far below there was dense fire and smoke as far as he could see. Saint Peter said, in an almost threatening tone, "What do you think of that?"

"That's a big damn fire, and clearly out of control, but I tell you what, we got some ol' boys down in Houston who can put that out for ya."

RANCHERS' CONVENTION

This is a story I classify as urban folklore. I first heard it 40 years ago, and this is my own version of it.

They had a convention of major landowners — big farmers and ranchers, some developers — up there in Denver. There were four men sittin' around in the bar in the fancy resort, enjoying happy hour. Three of them were swappin' stories about their farms and ranches and generally braggin' about their land holdings.

A fourth man, a Texan, was sittin' off to the side a bit. You knew he was from Texas because of the Lone Star hatband on his Stetson. He wasn't much involved in the conversation, just readin' the paper and half-listenin' to the others.

One of the talkers said, "I have about 8,122 acres of land along the western slopes of the Rockies here in Colorado. Have over 1,000 horses, I bet, if I could ever manage to count 'em all. Probably the highest ranch in the western U.S. We call it El Cielo Ranch because it's so close to heaven."

Next man said, "Sounds real nice. I have kind of the opposite. I own El Diablo Farms in Southern California's Imperial Valley. Always hotter than the devil down there. But we have over 9,500 irrigated acres. It is a desert, but just add water and watch the miracles happen. We grow produce faster than you can harvest it. LIke a license to print money!" he said, laughing loudly.

Third guy said, "Well, I don't have nearly that much land, but what I have is fertile. I've got about 6,000 acres in the Willamette Valley. It's the largest dairy operation in Oregon. Over 3,000 registered Holstein cows. Scottish Dairies, it's called. Supply milk to half of Portland. Only problem is the Willa-mette River runs right down the middle of my acreage and makes navigating my own property difficult. It's a beautiful problem to have, though."

The Texan was still sittin' quietly, and then one of 'em says, "Hey, Tex, how about you? How much land do you have?"

He said, "Well, down in Texas it's considered unseemly to ask a man how much land he owns or how many head of cattle he runs. We talk about land in terms of sections, not acres, but, since you gentlemen revealed your cards, I guess I can oblige your curiosity.

"I suppose, all told," he said, lookin' up at the ceiling as though mentally counting, "I have 200 acres."

The three men burst out laughing. The Californian said, "Two hundred acres! What the hell you doin' here at this gathering? What do you call your little ranchito, Tex?"

And the guys laughed some more.

"Well," drawled the Texan, "I don't have a name for it myself, but people in Texas like to call it — downtown Dallas."

Things got mighty quiet.

The Texan drank the last swallow of his Shiner Bock, got up and said, "Any of you boys want to sell your land, let me know. I'll dip into my petty cash account and buy you out."

With that he tipped his Stetson politely, grinned and said, "Y'all have a nice evenin', now."

SHOW HIM YOUR BADGE

This story comes under the heading of a Texas classic. It is folklore. I don't know for sure that its origin is in Texas, but the oldest versions I know of, going back 30-plus years, have Texas linguistic markers. In any case, the story has migrated around the world. I've heard Australian versions and Irish versions, and I suppose if I ever go to China I'll hear a version translated from Mandarin. In Texas, the story goes like this:

A West Texas rancher was stacking some hay in his barn when he heard a truck rumble across his cattle guard, half a mile away. He looked up to see what looked like a Government Suburban — dark windows — trailing a caliche dust cloud boiling up behind it as it raced his way. He walked out in front of the barn to meet it, and it came to a quick halt right in front of him, sliding the last five feet.

A young man hopped out. Slacks, pressed shirt. Glock on his hip. Badge on his belt.

"Can I help you?" rancher asks.

"Sir, I'm a law-enforcement officer," the young man said, pointing to his badge. "Just making a courtesy stop to let you know that we have word of drug activity in this area. I'm going to be looking around your ranch for a couple of hours to either confirm or invalidate these reports."

"Well," said the rancher, looking mystified. He pushed his salt-stained hat back off his forehead. "Ain't no drugs around here except the big ol' horse pills my doctor gives me for my rheumatism," he said, chuckling.

"This is not a laughing matter, sir. I assure you this is serious official business."

The rancher said, "I'm sure it is. Go ahead. Help yourself, son. Just don't go in that 20 acres behind the barn."

The officer got visibly angry for a second, his face reddening and his chest puffing out. He thrust his chin forward at the rancher.

"Sir," he said, "You see this badge? This badge gives me unimpeded authority, granted by the U.S. Constitution, to go where I please, when I please — no questions asked. I will decide where I will and won't go. Do you understand me, sir?"

"Sure do," the rancher replied, "I'll guess I'll just get back to stackin' my hay."

"Wise choice. That would be best," said the officer, as he strode away.

The rancher had been stacking hay for about five minutes when he heard a bloodcurdling scream from the pasture behind the barn.

Rushing around the barn, the rancher observed the agent running for his life, a scant five yards ahead of the rancher's big longhorn bull. He couldn't tell which one would arrive at the fence first, the agent or the bull.

Spotting the rancher, the officer yelled: "Help me! Call him off! What do I do?" The rancher cupped his hands to his mouth and yelled, "Show him your badge!"

HOLIDAYS
AND OBSERVANCES

CHRISTMAS: COWBOYS ON CANVAS

This is the story of a boy who loved Christmas so much that he grew up to make it more magical for the rest of us.

The boy grew up to be an artist, and his name is Jack Sorenson. He spent his childhood on the edge of Palo Duro Canyon, a place so rare in its quality of light that Jack's unique talents must have been uniquely nurtured.

Jack was drawing before he remembers doing it. His mother told him that, when he was 3, he would put the dog on the couch so he could make a sketch and then get terribly frustrated when his canine model would not hold a pose. By the time he reached first grade, he was so proficient at drawing whatever he saw that his teacher called his mother to tell her she thought he was a prodigy. His mom had never heard the word, and at first she thought the teacher was telling her he'd been misbehaving. Once she understood, though, she said, "Oh, yes, he can draw anything."

I talked to Jack for about 30 minutes a while ago. He and I have some things in common. We are both of a similar generation, and we are both life-long Texans. We both live in one of the "corners" of Texas — he in Amarillo and me in Brownsville. We are both slow talkers because of our Texas drawls. Took us 30 minutes to have a 15-minute conversation.

But when it comes to art we are on different planets. When he was being called a prodigy, my first-grade teacher was looking at an eagle I had drawn freehand and noting that it was not a bad likeness of a chihuahua.

Jack, who was born in 1954, says, "I've always been able to draw, sketch and paint anything I put my mind to. I didn't just discover it one day. I've always had it. God blessed me with a gift, and I try to honor that gift as best I can, in every painting."

It's not surprising that Western scenes are what Jack is known for. When he was growing up, his dad ran a Western-themed tourist town and dude ranch called Six Gun City on the rim of the Palo Duro Canyon. As a youth, Jack performed there, as a gunfighter and a stagecoach driver.

He liked to sketch the cowboys, but he soon found that cowboys didn't much care for portraits of themselves, or even of their girlfriends. He learned, however, that if he could capture the personality or the beauty and power of their horses, they would always buy that drawing. So he drew pictures of horses and sold them at $40 apiece.

As a result, Jack learned how to draw a horse with great accuracy and authenticity. Among aficionados of Western art, many say no one can paint a horse like Sorenson — no one alive, anyway. According to Jack's father, first there was Frederic Remington, then there was Charles Russell, then Jack Sorenson.

Have you ever noticed that if a photograph is exceptional people say it looks like a painting and if a painting is exceptionally realistic they say it looks like a photograph? Some of Jack's paintings look very much like photographs. I asked him if he ever painted from a photograph and he said, "No. A photograph will lie to you." If you try to paint a horse from a photograph, he said, your dimensions will be wrong. The head will be too big for the body, for instance.

"A camera can't get the truth of a horse," he said, "but a painting can."

Of his own paintings, Jack says, "each painting is a story in still form." It is true. I enjoy reading the stories in his paintings. One, for example, shows a cowboy in the midst of a bath in a river. Something has just spooked his horse, and our bathing cowboy looks alarmed as he sees his mount running off with his recently shed clothes flapping beneath the saddle.

One of Jack's Christmas paintings tells of a mounted cowboy arriving home late in the evening, Christmas Eve, perhaps. His daughter, maybe 6 years old, has been watching for him and, having seen his approach, has burst out of the house, run down the front steps and into the snow-covered road to greet her daddy. Behind her is a white frame house decked in icicles, with lamplight illuminating the windows and wood smoke escaping the chimney. Behind her daddy's back, his gloved hand holds a brown-haired doll that looks a good deal like his daughter. The excited little girl looks so happy to see her dad, but she's gonna be even happier in just a minute.

Jack loves Christmas. He says no one loves Christmas as much as he does. When he was a boy, he always wanted to be the one to pick the Christmas tree. His father would send him down into Palo Duro Canyon to select one. He'd cut a big one and drag it back to the house behind the horse, often through the snow. This scene would find its way into a painting, as would one of a boy balanced precariously on his saddle as he tries to get a Christmas star on top of a snow-covered pine tree.

At some point, Jack started painting Western Santas. Santa on horseback, Santa sledding down a snowdrift, Santa driving a stagecoach overflowing with toys. These Santa paintings have become a signature of the Colorado-based Leanin' Tree Christmas cards, which counts Jack's cards among its best-sellers.

His paintings have also been featured on a number of magazine covers. And, if you want an original, Jack sells his oil paintings at Joe Wade Gallery in Santa Fe, New Mexico — one of those places where, if you have to ask the price, you can't afford it.

The first Christmas paintings I saw by Jack made me think of him as a Western Norman Rockwell. His cowboys are so lovingly defined against a harsh winter background; his Santas have slightly cherubic

Reprinted with permission of Jack Sorenson

'The Homecoming,' by Jack Sorenson.

cheeks and sit a horse with more seasoned agility than a city Santa could. I love being surrounded by Sorenson's works over the holidays. His paintings make me think of simpler times, when a doll in a blue dress, delivered on horseback on a snowy Christmas Eve, could be the greatest gift in the world.

Jack knew early in life, when he was a teenager, in fact, that his life would be lived as a painter. In his seventh decade, he feels he is still improving:

"I'm in exactly the right spot at exactly the right time, and I'm doing what God wants me to do. You can't ask for more than that."

CHRISTMAS: HOW TO BAKE AN APPLE PIE

Every Christmas my mom would bake eight pies, four apple and four pecan. Now, we wouldn't eat all of those ourselves. Two would be given away to pie-less people, and two would be placed in the deep-freeze for some emergency of the future. Pies and money were similar in my mom's mind: Save a fourth of everything in deep savings for some future deep need.

When baking these pies, she had a memorable ritual.

First she would prepare the dessert table in the dining room. She'd cover the corner table with her mother's crocheted tablecloth and light some red cinnamon-scented candles. She'd tell us, every year, "See this tablecloth? Took your grandmother a year to crochet it. She made the whole thing while watching *Gunsmoke*."

Next she'd put on some Christmas music on the old phonograph. Usually Bing Crosby or Perry Como or Doris Day. Then she'd close off the kitchen and announce to any of us kids in there:

"I'm going to bake now. You're either a help or a hindrance. If you're gonna help, help. If not, get on outside."

I'd generally stay because there were rewards to be had. I served as quality control. At the age of 9, I found that just sitting in the warm kitchen amidst the aromas of baking pies had no olfactory equal in childhood.

My mom always cooked kind of dressed up. She wore a collared, mid-shin-length dress with a blue-and-white checked apron over it. This made her look, to me, like a Butter Krust bread wrapper, or like Betty Crocker without the pearls and without the little low heels. She'd be wearing a comfortable pair of beige Keds instead.

Now, as I was partial to her apple pie, I'm gonna tell you, right quick, how to make it like she did. And you should feel honored, because this is a treasured family recipe going back to my grandmother, who lovingly snipped it from the pages of *Good Housekeeping* magazine in 1912.

First you need to put some wassail on the stove to give the room the proper Christmas aroma for pie baking. Next you're gonna need a Formica table with a blue broken-ice pattern and chrome trim. Cover half the table with wax paper, get out your flour and rolling pin and make some pie crusts. Go about it vigorously so there's flour floating in the air. Line your pie dishes with the dough, snip off the excess, push in the crimps around the edges, and pop 'em all in the oven for 15 minutes at 350 degrees.

Now, if you're like my mom, never one to waste time, while those are baking, you can grab a 9-year-old boy and rush out to the clothesline and bring in the laundry, fold it and put it away before the pie crust is ready.

Back to the pies. Peel and core five Granny Smith apples. Cut into slices. Yell for your husband to turn the record over so you can hear Bing Crosby dreaming of a white Christmas, which is certainly a crazy thing to be dreaming about anywhere south of Austin. You're more likely to get a Christmas tan.

In a big stainless-steel bowl, mix the sliced apples, white and brown sugar, cinnamon and nutmeg all together. Nutmeg is the secret ingredient. Smells magical all mingled with the wassail warmed up on the stove. Now pour this filling into the pie shells and add a crumb topping that has lots of butter and sugar and cinnamon. You're almost done with your Dutch apple pies. All that's left is the baking. When they're done, set 'em up by there by the screened window to cool.

Now you can get started on the pecan pies, but that's not my specialty, so you'll have to look up that recipe. I'm just waiting for the apple pies. As soon as they cool, I'm gonna try a slice, with some Blue Bell Homemade Vanilla Ice

Cream, of course. Life doesn't get much better, I'd say.

May your holidays be equally blessed.

Here is my mother's recipe, exactly as written:

MARY BESS STRONG'S APPLE PIE

Place one pie crust in oven and bake at 350 for 15 minutes
Remove from oven and wait until it is cool to the touch
6 Granny Smith apples — peel and slice
2 heaping spoons of flour
1/2 cup of sugar
1 ts ground nutmeg
Mix and fold in sliced apples and pour evenly into pie shell.

TOPPING

1 stick butter at room temp.
1/2 cup dark brown sugar
Combine the sugar with the butter
1/2 teaspoon cinnamon
1 cup flour cut into butter and sugar to make crumb crust
spread over filling
Bake at 400 for 10 minutes and lower heat to 350 and cook 40-50 min.
Results may vary.

VETERANS DAY: NISEI, HONORARY TEXANS

I was looking at a list of honorary Texans recently. It is quite a long list. Only about a 10th of them would be known to most Texans.

John Wayne — no surprise there; the only surprise is that it took until 2015 to make him one. Chuck Norris, born in Oklahoma, was made an honorary Texan in 2017. Gov. Rick Perry made many of his favorite political allies honorary Texans: Rush Limbaugh, Sean Hannity, Sarah Palin and Glenn Beck, for example. George W. Bush, on the other hand, made Bob Dylan an honorary Texan. Ann Richards honored Don McLean, Bob Hope and Arnold Schwarzenegger, among many others. Alan Shivers made Gen. Douglas MacArthur an honorary Texan.

The one case that stands out to me as the most astounding in this honoring business, and to my mind the most deserving, is when Gov. John Connally, in 1962, awarded honorary Texan status to thousands of men simultaneously. He made the entire 442nd Regimental Combat Team and the 100th Infantry Battalion, C Divisions, of the U.S. Army from World War II, honorary Texans. With the help of Scott McGaugh's book *Honor Before Glory*, I thought I would tell you the story of how this came to be.

We must begin our story with the First Battalion of the 141st Infantry Regiment, drawn from the Texas National Guard. Their nickname became the "Alamo Regiment." In 1944, they were at the lead of the push to drive the Germans out of France. They had a large supporting force during their campaign, but they pushed ahead so fast in the Vosges Mountains so fast that they found themselves cut off and surrounded behind enemy lines.

The only good thing for the Texans is that they were on top of a mountain and had the classic advantage of high ground and line of sight. But they were still pounded by German artillery. It was foggy, rainy and cold. They quickly dug fighting positions in the wet, muddy soil and covered themselves with tree limbs, rocks and dirt. They did everything they could to provide cover from the splinters of trees hit by artillery and shrapnel from exploding shells. But they were also running out of food and water. A few exceptionally courageous pilots were able to fly through the rain and fog to airdrop supplies of water purification pills, C-rations and ammunition, but most of these missed their mark and went to the Germans instead.

The Army redirected its push to the Rhine to focus on saving the First Battalion from the Germans. American forces pounded the German lines with their artillery, but the forest was so thick they weren't having much effect. Two different infantry battalions were deployed to try to break through the German lines, but each was repelled by hailstorms of bullets from the German machine guns the soldiers called Hitler's buzz saws.

That was when the 442nd and the 100th infantry combat regiments were called in. They had a reputation for succeeding in just these situations. Their motto was "Go for Broke." It took them five days of brutal, close-quarters combat on muddy terrain in bone-chilling weather to reach the Texans. They fought tree to tree and yard by yard to reach the top of the mountain. The 442nd started out with 3,000 men and suffered 1,000 casualties: 800 wounded, 200 killed in action.

By the time the two regiments reached them, the Texans' numbers, too, had been fairly devastated. More than 20 percent of them had been killed, wounded or captured. Thanks to the fierceness of the 442nd and the 100th, though, after almost a week of besiegement they were freed from the German onslaught. It is said that the first soldier of the 442nd to reach them merely walked up to their commander, Lt. Marty Higgins, nonchalantly pulled out his Lucky Strikes and said, "Cigarette?"

What makes this story all the more surprising is not just the ferocity with which the 442nd fought or the casualties they took to save their brothers in arms: The real surprise is that the 442nd was a Nisei regiment, made up of second-generation Japanese-Americans, volunteers from Hawaii and the mainland. Most of them, along with their families, either had been put into internment camps at the beginning of the war or feared they would soon be moved to such camps. The men of the 442nd, however, had enlisted rather than sit out the war. The 100th Infantry Battalion, for its part, was made up primarily of Japanese-American members of the Hawaii National Guard; it had seen heavy combat before merging with the 442nd as a single combat unit.

These men were extraordinary fighters. The 442nd was called the Purple Heart Regiment because its members received more Purple Hearts than any other unit their size in WWII. Over the course of the war, soldiers from the 442nd was awarded 5,200 Bronze Star medals, 588 Silver Stars, 52 Distinguished Service Crosses, seven Distinguished Unit Citations and 21 Congressional Medals of Honor. The late Sen. Daniel Inouye was one of the Nisei who fought to rescue the Texans and later earned his Medal of Honor when he lost his arm taking out a German machine-gun nest in Italy.

When the 442nd returned from Europe, President Truman addressed the troops in Washington, D.C. He said, "You fought not only the enemy, but you fought prejudice — and you have won. Keep up that fight, and we will continue to win — to make this great republic stand for just what the Constitution says it stands for: the welfare of all the people all the time."

Many years after the war, President Clinton upgraded a good number of the military awards for the 442nd. Clinton observed that some of the Nisei had not received their due because they were Nisei, saying, "Rarely has a nation been so well-served by a people so ill-treated."

And that is why Gov. Connally, too, paid tribute to the 442nd and the 100th Battalion by making them all honorary Texans. It was his way of demonstrating to these soldiers, and their descendants, the solemn gratitude of the state of Texas, which will always be grateful for the supreme sacrifice they made in saving our men.

FOR FURTHER READING: *Much of the background for this commentary was provided by Scott McGaugh's splendid book* Honor Before Glory.

HALLOWEEN: *THE TEXAS CHAINSAW MASSACRE,* REANIMATED

Texas is No. 1 in a great many things: oil, ranching, rodeo, cotton. But you may be surprised to know that we also have a claim on No. 1 in horror. That's right, our very own charming little low-budget film *The Texas Chainsaw Massacre* is considered by many critics to be their favorite (and most horrifying) horror movie ever made.

At the time of its release in 1974, the famous film critic Rex Reed said that it was the most terrifying movie he had ever seen. The celebrated master of horror Wes Craven recalls wondering "what kind of Mansonite crazoid" could have produced such a thing. Stephen King called it a feat of "cataclysmic terror." And my favorite critique comes from the erudite Oxonian film critic and connoisseur of the macabre Anton Bitel, who said that the very fact that it was banned in England was a tribute to its artistry.

In honor of Halloween, I thought I would help you appreciate this hallowed film by sharing with you a few things you may not know about *The Texas Chainsaw Massacre.*

• Ed Gein is the name of the real criminally insane killer who inspired the character of Leatherface. He did not wear a leather mask. What he wore was worse: a mask made of human skin.

• Gein did his killing in Wisconsin, not Texas. I know, *Wisconsin Chainsaw Massacre* just doesn't have the same poetic ring to it.

• Ed Gein confessed to the killings of two people, not dozens (though he was suspected in several other unsolved murders and disappearances). He did not use a chainsaw. He used a gun.

• So where did the chainsaw idea come from? Tobe Hooper, the Texas-born director, says it came from a thought he had in a Montgomery Ward store in Austin a few days before Christmas. The store was annoyingly crowded with aggressive shoppers. As he stood in front of the chainsaws he had a disturbing epiphany. He realized that if he started up one of those chainsaws the sound alone would part that sea of shoppers, giving him a quick path to the exit. And that, ladies and gentlemen, is how iconic art is born.

• One last thing about Gein, also known as the Butcher of Plainfield. He was the inspiration not only for Leatherface but also for Norman Bates in *Psycho* and Buffalo Bill in *Silence of the Lambs.* Gein not only cut up the bodies of the women he shot but dug up corpses from graves, skinned them and dissected them for parts.

• For the actors, perhaps the most horrifying aspect of *The Texas Chainsaw Massacre* was that it was filmed in the middle of the scorching Texas summer. You can see the sweat dripping — even streaming — off the actors. Hooper's tight timeline did not allow for him to wait till cooler weather.

• In his much-praised book, *Chain Saw Confidential: How We Made the World's Most Notorious Horror Movie,* Gunnar Hansen, who played the character of Leatherface, said that the name of the depraved family in the first film is Slaughter, not Sawyer. If you look at the Coca-Cola sign over the gas station you will see "W. E. Slaughter BARBECUE."

• Hansen also noted that the power of the chainsaw myth they created on film persists with such tenacity in Texas that people would not believe him when he told them no such chainsaw crimes ever happened in the state. People would say something like: "No, they happened. My cousin worked on death row over in Huntsville and saw Leatherface himself get the chair." After all, the film did market itself as "based on a true story."

• The film cost less than $300,000 to make and eventually grossed $30 million in the United States.

• The movie had its opening in Austin, appropriately, since that's where it had been filmed (well, mostly near Round Rock, actually, as well as Bastrop) and where its director had grown up.

• Though it may be hard to believe, Hooper had intended to keep the gore and violence of the film to a minimum so he could get a PG rating. Didn't work. He got an R rating — escaping an X rating only after cuts and revisions.

• You can actually dine at two of the film's emblematic locations:

The old Victorian hippie house in Williamson County that was home base for the film was dismantled and moved to the grounds of the Antlers Hotel in Kingsland, where it is now the Grand Central Café.

The film's "Last Chance Gas Station," in Bastrop, was repurposed a few years ago as the Gas Station, with a barbecue café (complete with Coca-Cola sign declaring "WE SLAUGHTER BARBECUE), cabins, a campground and a gift shop with *Chainsaw* tchotchkes and souvenirs from the film. I understand the barbecue ain't half bad. At least the owners are not, like those in the film, focused only on serving their fellow man.

— Co-written by Alexandra Seymour

MOTHER'S DAY: QUANAH PARKER

That he rarely lost a battle to soldiers who relentlessly pursued him . . .

That he and the Quahada Comanches whom he led were as elusive as ghosts to pursuers on the High Plains . . .

That many chroniclers have described him as handsome, with the kind of looks that could grace the cover of one of those steamy Western romance novels . . .

That he was the last Comanche chief to decide on his own to move to the reservation, and thereafter worked with the whites toward self-sufficiency for his people . . .

. . . is not the point of this commentary.

This is a love story, but not a love story for Valentine's Day. This is a love story more appropriate for Mother's Day.

Quanah Parker's mother, Cynthia Ann Parker, was abducted by Comanche raiders on the Texas frontier when she was 9 or 10, in 1836. She was raised as a Comanche and was taken as his mate by a warrior, Peta Nocona. She had three children, Quanah, born in either 1845 or 1852, according to conflicting accounts; a younger son, Pecos; and a daughter, Topsanna, or Prairie Flower. Though attempts were made by white traders to recapture or trade for her, and her family organized a ransom offer once they received word that she had been seen among the Comanches, she never voluntarily returned to white society. Though born white, she was now culturally Comanche, the mate of a warrior, with three children she loved.

In 1860, a force of Texas Rangers under Lawrence Sullivan Ross attacked a Comanche camp along a tributary of the Pease River in West Texas. Three captives were taken, among them a woman with blue eyes and an infant daughter. Cynthia Ann was finally freed from captivity, but she saw it as being abducted again. She was now around 34, and she was uncertain of the fate of her husband and her boys. While being escorted to Tarrant County after the battle, she was photographed in Fort Worth with her daughter at her chest and her hair cut short, a Comanche sign of mourning. Both boys, however, had escaped. And, though Ross reported that his men had killed Peta Nocona, Quanah Parker himself said later that his father survived that raid and died four years later of natural causes.

She was kept at first with her uncle in Birdville, near Fort Worth, and then moved to live with other relatives in east Texas. But Cynthia Ann Parker never readjusted to white culture. She tried to escape and return to her tribe. She begged to go back to her people. As S.C. Gwynne reported in his masterpiece *Empire of the Summer Moon*, Cynthia Ann knew Spanish better than English. She told a translator: "*Mi corazón llorando todo el tiempo por mi dos hijos*" — "My heart cries all the time for my two boys."

Her relatives refused to consider the possibility that she belonged with the Comanches rather than with them and assumed she would readjust in time. In truth, she was being held captive a second time. She never gave up her Comanche ways. Her daughter died, possibly of influenza, a few years after they were returned to white society, in late 1863 or early 1864. And Cynthia herself died some seven years after that — according to some reports, she had stopped eating or drinking — still in her 40s.

Gwynne eulogized her this way: "She was a white woman by birth, yes, but also a relic of the Comancheria, of the fading empire of high grass and fat summer moons and buffalo herds that blackened the horizon. She had seen all of that death and glory. She had been a chief's wife. She had lived free on the high infinite plains as her adopted race had in the very last place in the North American Continent where anyone would ever live or run free. She had died in the deep pine woods where there was no horizon . . ."

Quanah had lost his mother when he was just 12 and longed for her all his life. After he surrendered to life on the reservation, he searched for her and learned that she had died and was buried far away in Texas. All he had of her was a photograph someone gave him, which he kept over his bed always.

He tried for many years to get her body moved and buried on Comanche soil. In 1910, he succeeded in having the bodies of his mother and his sister removed from East Texas and moved to Post Oak Mission Cemetery, at Cache, Okla., in Comanche County. The next year, he would be buried there as well. Their bodies were to undergo one last disruption in 1957, when the U.S. Air Force forced the removal of the cemetery for a missile base expansion and had the bodies moved to Fort Still Post Cemetery in Lawton, Okla. They remain there, together.

FOR FURTHER READING: Empire of the Southern Moon, *by S.C. Gwynne.*

VALENTINE'S DAY: VALENTINE, TEXAS, 2017

In Texas we have a lot of towns with cool names. There is actually a town named Cool. And Cut and Shoot. And Valentine. Yes, Valentine. How cool is that? Especially if it's February.

Photo by Mahala Guevara

The story goes that a Southern Pacific railroad crew, building eastward in 1882, had finished laying the tracks to the point where a water and fuel depot would be needed. It was Valentine's Day. So they named the depot Valentine. (There's also the possibility it was named for a Southern Pacific shareholder, John Valentine, who was the president of Wells Fargo, but that's no fun.)

Valentine, to give you coordinates, is halfway between L.A. and New Orleans, almost exactly 1,000 miles from each. Or, if you want something local, halfway between Marfa and Van Horn, in Jeff Davis County west of Fort Davis. Deep in the heart of West Texas.

Valentine never got very big. It says 217 on the city limits sign, but the mayor there, Jesus Calderon (who goes by Chuy), says the number is likely about 180 these days. Chuy has been mayor there for 40 years, possibly a record of some kind for mayoral longevity in Texas. In addition to being mayor, he taught in the Valentine Independent School District for decades and even worked part-time for many years as the local FedEx delivery man. Nobody knows Valentine like Chuy. He says there is no gas station, no ATM and no crime.

The school, K-12, has about 40 students. Some years they only graduate five or six from high school. One year, not too long ago, they graduated two. Think about that. If you're the poorer student of the two, you are simultaneously in the bottom 50 percent of your class AND the salutatorian. Lisa Morton, who grew up there and is managing editor of the *Van Horn Advocate,* says her sister graduated alone. I said that must have been a lonely event and she said, "Oh, no, the whole town came out to celebrate her big day." Gotta love small towns.

And here's another hard-to-believe statistic Chuy told me when I talked to him in 2017: With only about 10 boys in the high school that year, he said, two were named Elvis. So they joked that they could never be sure that "Elvis has left the building" unless they left together.

Well, the town isn't so small that it doesn't have a post office. And in February they are busier than Santa's elves on Christmas Eve. This time of year they receive thousands of cards to be remailed bearing the Valentine postmark. (There is also a Valentine, Neb., and a Valentines, Va., that does the same thing.) The cards come to Texas from all over the United States and as many as 30 foreign countries. One year they postmarked and sent one along to the White House, to Chelsea Clinton.

Each year there is a design contest at the school, and the winner's "love logo" is used for that year's postmark. Imagine that. You can send your Valentine a Valentine from Valentine. Can't get much more romantic than that!

Unless you take your Valentine *to* Valentine on the 14th. Chuy says they have a big party each year, Valentine's in Valentine, underwritten by Big Bend Brewing Co. from nearby Alpine. One year, Jerry Jeff Walker played. The year before that, Joe Ely was there playing his famous song "Saint Valentine." The next year, 2017, the headliner was Little Joe y La Familia.

That year Valentine's Day fell on a Tuesday, and there was pressure to move it to the weekend, but, as Mahala Guevara, vice president of operations at Big Bend Brewing, explained in the official brochure: "West Texas was never known for convenience; to enjoy the best the region has to offer, you have to be willing to work for it. And your hard work will be rewarded with great Texas music . . ." Gotta love it. A work ethic embedded in leisure. A very Texas concept.

Photo by Mahala Guevara

The late accordionist Anthony Ortiz Jr. and bassist Joey McGill with the band Crooks at the 2015 Valentine's in Valentine.

Big Bend Brewing even brewed a special ale for the event, called Total Commitment. At 14.2 percent proof, it is appropriately named. Makes my eyes a little misty thinking about it.

Really, though, Valentine seems to me to be a good place for romance. On nights when the moon is full, it turns half the sky to gold. Even on moonless nights, the stars are so bright that you can see a hint of your shadow. Under such a sky you slide into a gracious silence.

The most romantic Texas couple I know is Coach Taylor and his wife Tami, from *Friday Night Lights*. They are fictional, but they're also authentically romantic. I could see them taking an impromptu road trip to Valentine for Valentine's — just 200 miles from Dillon.

Coach Taylor always told his team: "Clear eyes, full hearts; can't lose." It's good advice for football. Probably good advice for love, too.

VALENTINE'S DAY: MY VALENTINE

At 60 I didn't expect ever to fall in love again. I thought the sort of euphoric madness that comes with infatuation was all in the past — reserved for younger people. But I was wrong. When *she* came into my life, the world stopped — and changed forever.

I first saw her in photographs. Someone showed me pictures — black-and-white, grainy photos. She was interesting, but the pictures didn't do her justice. When I finally met her in person, though, I thought she was the most beautiful creature I had ever seen. I was mesmerized. She was 7 ½ pounds and 19 inches of perfection.

At 60, she was my first little girl. Perhaps not a bona-fide miracle, but for me she was. My eternal valentine.

We named her Scarlett, for the feisty nature of Scarlett O'Hara in *Gone With the Wind,* and Paloma-Maria, after her two grandmothers.

That very night I began keeping a journal for her.

I wrote: *You are just a day old now. You are my ONLY girl, which makes you precious beyond measure. I will keep this little journal of our first years together. I will tell you what amazed you and what delighted you. Your first words will be here. Your first steps. I will do all I can, as will your mama, to make sure you are exposed to all the influences that will make you an extraordinary woman — one who is intellectually curious, adventurous, brave, full of self-confidence, but also empathetic and kind, a woman who is strong and gentle, too, both a warrior and a poet.*

Three years have passed now. People have started asking me how raising a girl, at least for me, is different from raising boys. I say, "Don't know much, but let me tell you what I didn't know."

Until I had a girl, I didn't know about spontaneous politeness and gratitude. Returning from the beach one day, she said, all on her own, "Thank you for taking me to the beach, Dada."

Until I had a girl I didn't have a child who thought I had super-powers. She handed me scissors and a piece of paper and said, "Can you make me a bicycle?" I said, "How about a rectangle?"

Until I had a girl I didn't know you had to dance to the opening theme songs of *Dora the Explorer* and *Elena of Avalor*. Scarlett's motto seems to be "Never miss a chance to dance."

Until I had a girl it was I who'd sung the lullabies. But she's not pleased with the way I sing them, so she often takes over.

Until I had a girl I didn't know that when you took her for a walk around the neighborhood in her big stroller, you had to take her dolls, too — all of them. I didn't know that dolls left behind would be sad.

Until I had a girl I was never awakened by a voice singing so sweetly: "Happy birthday to you, happy birthday to Dada . . ." I couldn't have been any more moved if it had actually been my birthday. Such technicalities don't matter to her, though. People need to celebrate their birthdays at least once a month, according to Scarlett's philosophy — to appreciate the simple joy of just being alive.

Until I had a girl I didn't know there were so many colors in the world. She has 300 around her easel. She likes to paint vermilion crocodiles.

Until I had a girl I never got my nails painted. One day she got her mom's polish and wanted to give me a manicure. I resisted. My wife shot me that "Don't be a Neanderthal" look. "OK," I said, "one hand." I forgot about it until later that afternoon, when I suddenly realized I was probably the only guy at the gun show with Autumn Mist nails. A man at one of the displays noticed my manicure as I was examining the merchandise and shot me a look. "Three-year-old," I explained. He grinned and leaned over with some advice: "Next time — go camo."

Until I had a girl I never had a child so empathetic. She wants to know how I'm feeling, if I'm happy or sad, or if anything hurts and if I might need a doctor — and, lucky for me, she happens to be one.

Until I had a girl I never had a child so young who was so self-aware. I asked her if she was Mama's girl or Dada's girl. She said, "I'm Scarlett's girl."

Until I had a girl I didn't know that Valentine's Day was so important. It's her favorite holiday, along with Christmas, Easter, Halloween, Thanksgiving and July Fourth. But truly, with her loving heart, Valentine's was made for her. A week before the holiday, she'd already popped the question: "Dada, will you be my Valentine?"

Yes, always and forever. And your mama's, too. After all, she did give me you. *When I recorded this piece for broadcast on* Texas Standard, *I brought Scar-*

lett along with me to the studio so she could demonstrate some of her singing. You can hear it here: **http://www.texasstandard.org/stories/my-valentine-a-life-changing-theme-song-singing-nail-painting-love/**.

Photo by Lupita Strong

TEXAS FAMILY MEMORIES

UNCLE DALE'S GREATEST GIFT

When I was growing up, most of the men went off to work in the morning and came home in the late afternoon or early evening. In our neighborhood, Uncle Dale was the first grown-up to come home every afternoon.

Uncle Dale lived across the road and a few houses down from us. He wasn't our real uncle. We just called him that. In those days and in towns like mine, everybody in the neighborhood knew each other and socialized in the evenings, especially in summer. We knew and spent time with most of the grown-ups who lived around us. "Mr." would have been too formal, but it was considered rude for a child to call an adult by his or her first name alone, so we had lots of aunts and uncles.

Uncle Dale got up when it was still dark and walked a mile to work, where he put in hard days at the local Halliburton yard. At 3:30 in the afternoon, he would walk back, like those "men in tired blue shirts" in Indiana poet Philip Appleman's *Memo to the 21st Century* who "followed their shadows home to grass."

And there he would sit in his lawn chair, under the gauzy shade of a mesquite tree, and watch over us as we played baseball in the road.

It was a caliche road; hard and dusty in the dry times and a mass of cake-like mud when it rained. Home plate and second base were in the middle of the street, first base was in the Garcias' yard and third base was in Uncle Dale's yard.

Uncle Dale was our umpire. He would sit there drinking coffee from his big white mug, smoking one cigar after another. We could smell that sweet tobacco drifting through the infield. Even now I can smell it as it drifts across the years to where I sit.

Uncle Dale ruled on close calls from the comfort of his place in the shade. "That was a foul," he'd say. Or he would coach: "Two hands while learning, R.J." He also served as traffic cop: "You boys get out of the road 'fore that truck runs over you."

I can remember his getting out of his chair only once. We were having our own little baseball draft, the way we always did: hand over hand up the bat — you remember.

Well, Mrs. Anderson came over and suggested we draw numbers out of a hat, making one team out of the even numbers and the other of the odd numbers, to spare the feelings of those often chosen last.

Uncle Dale would not stand for these progressive ideas. He was a purist. He got up and waved her off. He said, "If a boy is struggling, he needs to know it early so he can do something about it." We continued in our way.

One day when we came home from school, we saw Uncle Dale on a huge Halliburton bulldozer in the brush down the road. We went down there to watch him because, like all boys, we were fascinated with anything that could topple trees and remold the earth. After about 30 minutes of brush-clearing, he shut down the dozer, hopped off and said, "There's your new baseball field boys. You're off the streets." We were transfixed. "Well, don't just stand there," he said, "get your gloves, let's break her in!"

Never again was the crack of a bat muted by a car horn wanting to drive through our infield.

Uncle Dale's baseball field cost him a few phone calls and three hours of his expert labor, but it gave us, and the boys that followed us, years of immeasurable joy. It was the greatest gift we ever got, really — the gift of a beautiful boyhood, and the lifelong memory of it.

MOM

This tribute to my mother could also have been at home in the chapter about larger-than-life Texans. For me, that is what she was. Though a small woman, she was larger than life. And I think many of us had larger-than-life parents who made us the people we are.

My mom lived to be 101 and five months. I mention the five months because she said that once you reached 99 you started counting your age as if you were a newborn baby, in months: 99 and two months, 99 and six months, 99 and nine months. Her advice for those who wanted to live to be 100 was that you should live to be 99 and then be very, very careful.

My mom out riding in the evening at Mills-Bennett Ranch south of Falfurrias in 1960.

Mary B. Strong, whose name doubled as her motto, was a tough, no-nonsense woman. A Daughter of the American Revolution, survivor of the Great Depression; an honest-as-the-day is long woman of the Texas soil. Her maternal grandfather's name was Reuben "Pony" McGee. They called him Pony because he was always on the move. True to his reputation, once he had his family settled in Krum, Texas, in the late 1800s, he left for Oregon and never returned. Her father's family (his name was Fred Barnett) goes back to a signatory on the Texas Declaration of Independence and ultimately to Tennessee and West Virginia. This was a common migration pattern for the Scots and Scots-Irish out of the Appalachian region to Texas. My mother's cousins ranched the family land in North Texas for more than a century. They recently created the Barnett Ranch Conservancy, protecting 1000 acres in western Denton County for all Texans to enjoy.

Mary B. Strong loved her Texas heritage. She was like the pioneer women whose DNA she inherited, thoroughly resilient. She had what John Wayne personified in *True Grit*. I think anyone who lives so long — one in about 40,000 — must have true grit.

So what was the secret to her longevity?

She was always willing to try new things; never one to say "I'm too old for that." She bought her first computer when she was 88. She was on the internet writing emails at 92 and had 115 Facebook friends when she died. She refused to let technology leave her behind. Even when her hands were gnarled by arthritis and she could no longer type, she would dictate her emails to those who would type for her. Just a few days before she passed, she was admiring my iPhone, saying, "Oh, I'm gonna buy one of those for myself." (She didn't care about the phone, really. She just saw the potential for a thousand pictures of grandkids conveniently carried in her purse.)

She never stopped moving. In her latter years, when she never seemed to slow down, I thought, "Death will never catch her." She mowed her own lawn until she was 85, and she never stopped gardening. When she was 99, I asked her what she would do if she could be 18 for a day, and she said, "Oh, I would RUN! I would get out on that Galveston beach and just run until I ran out of island."

She continued to do her own dishes and laundry right up to her last days. She went to church three times a week, rarely allowing illness to keep her away.

"I won't feel any worse at church," she'd say, "and I might feel better."

She was a saver. As a child of the Depression, she never wanted to face want again. So she saved voraciously and took advantage of good deals. I can remember visiting her in the summers, and sometimes at breakfast she would clap her hands together and announce: "Oh, the Astros won last night, so let's not forget to go to Dairy Queen and get our free slush."

But she was never a miser. Though she would often deny herself what she considered luxuries, she was always generous with others. Strangely, she saved more in her retirement years than she did in her 40 years of working, but she could never bring herself to buy stock. A certificate of deposit was the only investment she trusted.

She was courageous. For her 101st birthday, she was asking me to take her for a ride on my motorcycle. I told her I would have to strap her down with bungee cords, and she said that would be fine. She was always ready for the next adventure.

She ate pretty much what she pleased. Eggs and bacon, barbecue, cheeseburgers, Mexican food, a Coca-Cola every mid-morning and a bowl of Blue Bell before bed — Homemade Vanilla with chocolate syrup. Her only compromise was in portions, always small. And no alcohol at all.

She had great pride. Her measure of people was in whether they took pride in what they did and how they lived. Sometimes her standards could be a bit unfair, as with the time she visited Arizona and complained about the shabby lawns out there. I reminded her that it was a desert and she said, "But if they had pride, they'd have nice yards."

That was her central value, I suppose: Pride. She always said to me, "I don't care much what you do in life, just make sure you live a life you can be proud of." And if she didn't personally like something, like the new truck I'd bought, she'd say, "Well, it's not my kinda truck, but I'm proud of it for ya." She said that a lot about things: "I'm proud of it for ya."

And that pride she looked for in others was evident in her. For her 101st birthday, I took her to the hair salon, a place she still called "the beauty parlor." On the way home I told her how lovely she looked. She leaned over my way as if she were sharing a secret, and said, "You know, a lot of people think I look only about 90."

Not many women can say that.

Give your Mom a big bear hug today. Say the four words she cherishes most: "I love you, Mom."

MY GRANDMA'S HAIR

My grandmother made me a writer. I don't know if she made me a particularly good one, but she is responsible for nurturing my early love of reading and writing. Her name, to the family, was Nonnie.

Her given name was Eunice, but we called her Nonnie. My mother told me later that, in her family, all Eunices were Nonnies. Like Beth for Elizabeth, Nonnie was short for Eunice, which I never understood since they had the same number of letters and syllables.

Nonnie lived with us when I was little, until just before she died, at age

82. I was fortunate to have my Nonnie as my personal nanny until I entered the first grade. My earliest memories are of Nonnie taking me on field trips around the back yard to see butterflies and mockingbirds and ants building their great cities. She taught me to focus on details and patterns in all that I saw. She also read to me from classic children's books and the Bible.

And I watched her write all the time, long letters to family far away, in a beautiful cursive style. She was also a diarist, maintaining daily entries in her black journals, which I later discovered contained autobiographical memories and philosophical wanderings that were both historical and religious. She was a pious woman and said she was not afraid of anything but "bad company."

She had done such a good job tutoring me in reading and writing and basic math in those early years that the school wanted to start me out in the second grade. My father was against it, though, thinking that it would throw off my social development; since he was the superintendent, his say was the final one.

When I entered first grade, Nonnie was free of her nanny duties, and she did something that was both astonishing and beautiful. She bought an entire set of World Book Encyclopedias and announced that, since she never got to go to college, this would be her college education. She planned to read the entire set and believed that would be equivalent to a bachelor's degree at a good university.

I don't know if she ever read them cover to cover, but she did sit on the couch and read various volumes quite often in those years. My brothers and I perused them, too. For us they were like an early version of Google. We could just think of a subject and pull down the volume and learn all about it. The writing was strong, and there were stunning photographs that animated the writing. The "S" volume was especially worn, since we liked learning about ships, snakes and sports.

The next astonishing thing that Nonnie did was to buy a Smith-Corona electric typewriter. She banged out four novels set in Texas before she died. She sent them off to publishers under a male pseudonym — Sylvester Wimberley (she liked the name of the little Hill Country town) — thinking that would improve her chances. Like most would-be authors, she received many rejection slips.

I wish I could tell you that she was finally successful and had a best-seller, but that was not the case. When she died, her novels were found neatly stacked in large brown envelopes in her chest of drawers. I remember well that they were in the bottom drawer, right beneath the one where she kept the tablecloths she crocheted. My mother packed them up and put them in the attic.

No one thought about them for years, until I was in my 30s and wanted to take a look at them. When I asked my mom if she knew where Nonnie's old manuscripts might be, she said, "Oh, I think those were thrown away. Someone in the family was concerned that there were embarrassing family histories in them." Now, keep in mind that in my family's idea of "embarrassing" would hardly raise eyebrows in polite society. It would be something like allowing people to know that some in our family were often hungry during the Depression, perhaps calling into question the depth of our work ethic.

I was immediately outraged by such an attitude. What if Nonnie were a late-blooming Jane Austen and someone had casually disposed of works of genius? What if they were only rejected because they were "before their time"?

I went up into the attic and searched around through dusty boxes, old toys, Christmas decorations and ancient suitcases. And there, in the bottom of one of those suitcases, neatly strapped in, were five brown manila envelopes. I pulled one of the manuscripts out. It was brittle and yellowed but fully intact and readable. It was an exciting moment.

It took me a few days to read through most of these works and to realize that Nonnie was more of a diarist than a novelist. She was good in short bursts but had trouble sustaining the long narrative required of a novel. What I particularly enjoyed reading was the writing in her journals, which luckily were packed away with the book manuscripts.

From one of these, I will share what is to me a touching memory about her hair.

From my earliest memories my hair has been a subject of conversation. My father was the first to make me conscious of it. He thought it was beautiful. It was long and straight and heavy with a gold cast to it. My father would not let it be cut. Even as the younger girls were getting theirs cut, my father would not let me cut mine because he liked the length of the braid.

My grandmother was on her deathbed and mother had to take time about with her sisters caring for her. So my father took care of us and he had his say about how I should wear my hair. When I went to school the boys would make fun of it saying it was the color of molasses candy that had been pulled. I am not sure the golden tint was still in it then. The boys delighted in sticking the ends of the braids into their ink wells which earned them my angry retaliation.

When I was twelve I went outside with my grandfather McGee one summer day. I went out on the front porch with him just after sunup. He turned to talk to me and he stopped and said, "Eunice, I didn't know that your hair was such a pretty red." I laughed and said that it was just the sun shining through it and lighting it up like that. I never forgot that moment. I had had so few compliments in my life and I was to remember that one always. My grandfather would sometimes pass behind me at the supper table and run his rough hand over my hair. He didn't say anything, but I found it as comforting as a compliment.

Many years later, after I had married, I still kept my hair long and braided. It had become strawberry blonde. I wore it as a braid wrapped around my head. I took the pins [out] of my hair and wrapped the braid around my neck. It was as wide as a collar. Once I was wearing it that way when I went to call on Betty Graham and she asked me where I got a collar that so closely matched my hair. I told her it WAS my hair. She had to take it down to see the length of it and was surprised by its weight, too. I suppose that was the longest, and heaviest, it ever was.

Once when my niece Guy Ann was five years old and she and I were standing out in front of the Gunter Hotel in San Antonio waiting for my husband Fred, a strange woman came up to me and said, "Lady, did you know that your hair and that child's hair are exactly the same color?" I had not thought about it but when we got home Guy Ann wanted to see for herself. So she pulled my hair down and laid hers over it. Sure enough, you could not tell where mine ended and hers began. As the years went by Guy Ann's hair got a little darker and mine got ever lighter until it was blonde and white.

In 1963, when I was in my late 70s, I ran into Sam Black, a man I had not seen for fifty years. He greeted me with these words, "Well, Eunice, you have lost some of the gold in your hair!" Indeed I had.

Now that I am 80 years old, my hair is all white. White like new cotton. And I think it is lovely.

My grandmother wanted all her life to be published. I am happy to know that, now, she finally is.

ACKNOWLEDGEMENTS

Someone said long ago that teachers never know where their influence stops. Such is true of Mrs. Eunice Anderson, my fourth-grade teacher. She read *Tom Sawyer* and *Huckleberry Finn* to us in the lazy afternoons of that year. I was mesmerized. I didn't know who Mark Twain was, but I loved the way he told a story. From then on I was a reader. It helped that my parents created a home that was essentially a library we also lived in. Surrounded by the intoxicating world of books, I couldn't help but become a bibliophile, and no doubt that propelled me into the academic world in which I have thrived all my life.

For this collection I am indebted to the farmers and ranchers among whom I spent my formative years. They were gifted storytellers all. In a world before the internet and a milieu not dominated by newspapers or TV, stories told in person carried our knowledge, our morality, our practical wisdom, our inspiration and our humor. The medium was the message because the stories came infused with the ethos of the person doing the telling. I loved those times, and I mourn their passing, because too often now great stories are reduced to a meme on a phone, and what Twain called the "manner of the telling" is sacrificed to just the "matter."

I must also join two generations of students from Falfurrias, Texas, in praising Ms. Doris Jenkins, our iconic high-school English teacher. She was as tough as Churchill and as wise as Socrates. She lifted the collective literacy of our little town more than we can ever know. I think that, if someone wanted to erect a statue in her honor in Falfurrias, there would be no shortage of donations from the generations she inspired.

I am grateful for the world I grew up in, in Falfurrias, Texas, in the 1960s and '70s. It was like being raised in a Norman Rockwell painting — idyllic, protected, but free. Many of the stories in this book have their origins there in those golden years. My boyhood friends, like Gonzalo Garcia, who remains one of my closest friends to this day, and the Dorow kids and the McCall boys, helped me enjoy a childhood Huckleberry Finn would have loved.

In college, at Abilene Christian University, my buddy Greg Lowe and I worked together to develop radio dramas and satirical shows in the vein of *Saturday Night Live* for the campus radio station, KACU. We were just playing, and in that playfulness we developed a talent for creating narratives that sustained themselves. Now Dr. Lowe, Greg continues to inspire my creative work to this day.

In those years I also wrote a humor column for the school paper that taught me the discipline of delivering a weekly product and adapting my stories for a demographic that was essentially me. What could I tell them that they didn't already know? I found that the manner of the telling mattered.

I certainly want to thank my great professors like Dr. Rex Kyker at ACU and Dr. Ted Colson of the University of North Texas, who taught me to admire particularly the flow of a good story, and to appreciate, as with a beautiful dance, how it moves.

I have to apologize to my grad-school friends, Bob House, John Cook, Julie Patterson, Steve and Kathy Judice and many others who had to put up with all my storytelling and anecdotes about the latest author I had fallen in love with in those rich years of glorious poverty. I thank them now for their patience in letting me learn the difficult of art of how to tell a story well.

Dr. Jack Stanley pushed me to write on a consistent basis, teaching me that one cannot simply wait for the muse to strike because, without discipline, the muse's inspiration is wasted.

Dr. Juliet V. Garcia and Nikki Englitsch both have my sincerest gratitude for believing in the deep value of these stories before I did. They were my aesthetic life coaches who urged me on when I thought the well was dry.

My colleague of three decades, Dr. George McLemore, has been my finest stylistic critic. He has consistently read everything I've written, applauding the good and prescribing remedies for what was weak — always, as we say in South Texas, *con cariño* (with affection).

Leah Scarpelli, who for the past two years has been my editor at *Texas Standard Radio,* the daily public-radio news broadcast on which my stories air, has my sincerest gratitude. Her meticulous editing of my writing and my sound has improved me greatly. She has often saved me from disaster by catching significant errors in fact and grammar. I am most grateful for her fine work in polishing my sometimes-not-ready-for-NPR-style.

I thank this book's editor, Amy Culbertson, for the myriad e-mails and notes she wrote to me over six weeks of editing, pushing me hard to bolster, refine, support and amplify the stories so they would be stronger. I appreciate her experience, talent and saintly patience.

I owe Michael Ashby a few cases of Shiner Bock for his work on the photos. He graciously lent me his time and talent, digitally enhancing all the photos so that they would have the appropriate resolution in print. Texas has sublime landscapes, and he made sure we didn't lose that sublimity in translation between media.

Most of all, I thank my wife, Lupita, herself a voracious reader and lover

Photo by Larry White, Larry White Photography, Facebook

of the world's great novels. She has been my first editor and cheerleader and sometime savior, rescuing me from the brink of linguistic error and bad judgment. She has been my co-author at times and always my muse, my biggest fan and the one who often reminds me of my own maxim: "The greatest mistake in life is thinking it is too late."

No doubt there are people I should recognize and thank, but my memory is not what it once was and probably never was what I remember it to be. So, if I have forgotten you, I leave the space below so you can write yourself in and show it to others.

_____ was invaluable to the creation of this book.
— *W. F. Strong, 2018*

ABOUT THE AUTHOR

W. F. Strong is a Fulbright scholar and professor of communication at the University of Texas Rio Grande Valley. He grew up in South Texas and holds degrees in communication and literature from Abilene Christian University and the University of North Texas, as well as a doctorate in communication and rhetoric from the University of Arizona. His storytelling influences range from Mark Twain, on whom he wrote his doctorate dissertation, to former public-radio host Garrison Keillor.

Strong has pursued a lifelong fascination with Texas literature, history and culture, having immersed himself in the classic books of the great Texas novelists and historians, from Walter Prescott Webb's *Indians of Texas* to Larry McMurtry's *Lonesome Dove* series to Philipp Meyer's *The Son*.

He grew up working on farms and ranches in South Texas and so has had a long connection with the Texas soil, as did his ancestors, who farmed and ranched in North Texas for more than a century. Two of his distant forebears signed the Texas Declaration of Independence from Mexico. This familial history has nurtured his love for the vibrancy of Texas culture, both historical and modern.

All these influences came together in the development of a series of brief, often humorous, sometimes dramatic radio vignettes. Called *Stories From Texas,* they are intended to teach and amuse and inspire. In them he seeks to celebrate the Texas character in all its toughness; to showcase poignant passages from the vast literature this land has produced; and to provide a narrative for Texas pride, entrepreneurial success and Texas mythology. Celebrating Texas' charismatic culture and revealing the diverse forces that forged it, *Stories From Texas* airs biweekly on *Texas Standard Radio,* a daily news program produced in Austin that is carried on 30 NPR stations across Texas.